Foreword

In memory of my beloved Father and Mother
who said 'yes' to peace, love, respect and trust.
I cherish what you gave me.

Acknowledgements

My gratitude goes to Joan who kept me on the straight and narrow with patience and encouragement and helped me to finally complete my story.

A big thank you to my husband, Lolly, for our many interesting years together. I have always relied on your hard work and your love.

To my sons, Ian and Chris, I am particularly grateful for the joy you have brought to my life and your interest in building up Tshukudu and the farm at Ohrigstad.

To Sylvia, thanks for being such a good wife and mother and for the joy and happiness you have brought to our family, and to Sonja for the wonderful times we have had together.

To my grandchildren – Patrick, David, Stephen, Richard, Jessica and Matthew – thank you for the joy. I hope this book helps inspire you to lead full and honest lives.

To my family in Poland and to Lolly's family in South Africa – thank you for your continued support.

To all my friends – too many to mention by name – thank you for your support and the great times we have enjoyed together over the years.

Thanks to my great friend – and legal eagle – Derek Verster, as well as Seun and Wilma Beneke, for your tremendous help over and above the call of duty at Tshukudu; and also thanks to Marianne Wilding for the brilliant Tshukudu videos.

To my two special Polish friends, Renia and Katja, who have been like sisters to me over the years.

To the staff at Tshukudu for your loyalty and hard work – I am indebted also for the love you have put into the wildlife and the running of the lodge.

And, finally, to our regular clients who return to us time after time and have become our friends: thank you.

Part 1
Stolen Childhood
1930 - 1949

Good times

It was a cold day in hell.

How often had I heard those words said in jest. I laughed back then. Of course there was no such thing! Everybody knew that hell was hot. But this was now. Siberia at its best in summer is a miserable place. This was Siberia in winter at its worst. The women had cut squares of turf and piled them against the outside of the tents to try to keep out the cold. I suppose it helped, but not so as you would notice.

But I go too fast. It was not always like this. There were good times – oh such good times! Perhaps that's what made this the harder to bear – my early childhood had not prepared me for this pain and degradation.

I, Alina Kuchcinska, was born in Poland on the 6 June 1930 to the most wonderful parents you can imagine. In South Africa I am known as Ala and in Poland my name took on the diminutive form of Alutka. This is what my family called me. My home was filled with love.

Mother and Father's wedding, April 1929

My mother and father never fought. My father, Lubomir Kuchcinski, was a judge and he adored my mother. My mother, Maria Telatycka, was a kind, loving person.

We lived in a beautiful home in Swieciany, near Wilno in present-day Lithuania (although it was a part of Poland back then).

I had such a wonderful childhood. I have one brother, Janusz, who is two years younger than I. He was a bit naughty and mischievous from the moment he was born. He certainly did not take after my father who was a perfect gentleman, always regal in every aspect in his work and in his social life. I used to wonder how Janusz became part of my idyllic family. I remember saying to my mother, "You got the wrong baby. They must have changed him at the hospital!"

It's a peculiar thing, but in Poland if your father was a judge, his wife was called 'Mrs Judge'. I think it's a little bit crazy being so fussy about titles. Personally, I still don't like the idea. My mother used to be involved in a lot of social work. Right up to her death she was concerned about those who were less fortunate. She was a happy, social person and was loved by everyone. Our house was filled with laughter and merriment. Her sunny face belied the hardships she had experienced as a young girl. As a student during the first world war she lived on an estate. The estate was burnt to the ground by the Russians. She and her family were taken to Siberia. It must have been a hard time for her, but she seldom talked about it. Her life changed after she married my father.

Years later, in Africa, she once told me, "You know, your father adored me.

Father

Mother

He never fought with me; he was never nasty to me, not like you are sometimes! I never knew hardship; I never endured hard words; I was always adored. I was his princess in every respect."

As a child in Poland I had a nanny named Emilia. She was a wonderful person and was treated as a friend and a member of our family rather than as a servant. With my mother there were never any barriers.

Our home was huge but everything always seemed to be done. There was food on our table and we were well cared for without any stress. We did not have dishwashers or washing machines to help with the chores, but we had lots of dinner parties. It was an industrious household – apples were packed in the cellar where my father made his own wine and mother stored her homemade jam.

Playing bridge was a much-loved pastime for my parents. They also enjoyed kayacking and swimming. The lakes near where we lived afforded many wonderful family weekends. In fact everything contributed to make mine a dream childhood.

The winters were severe in Swieciany, the hills covered in snow. Going to school was an adventure. We would race down the hills on our skis and travel through forests on horse-drawn sleighs. When he was small, baby brother Janusz would sleep snugly under a blanket.

Two childhood memories are indelibly etched on my mind. When I was about six years old I spent a holiday with my aunt on an estate near Bialystok. One night lightening struck a storeroom full of hay and there was a huge fire. I was left alone in the house because all the adults ran to try to save the barn, and they said that I had to stay inside. I had never been left alone like this before. All I could see from the window was a huge ball of fire, intensified by the reflection in a dam which fronted the house. The dry hay exploded in vivid orange flames. Many people suffered burns trying to save the building. Injured people came into the house. My helplessness was overwhelming. I ran around in confusion saying, "What do I do? Where do I look for plasters?"

From that day I have been very frightened of lightening – it reminds me of the fire and the injured people. I still shudder at the sound of thunder and often find myself in silent prayer during an electric storm, "Oh my God, don't let it strike us," and yet I pray for rain.

My other memory is a much happier, although poignant, one: Christmas time. It was a very special time for our family. The start was the Christmas evening meal – the *Wigilia*. We all joined in the exciting preparation which was a build-up to the big event. We tried not to eat too much during the day, which was a Polish custom, to make sure that we had plenty of room for the feast that was to come. We put hay onto our dining table which we covered with a white cloth. The reason for the hay was to celebrate Jesus' birth in a crib filled with hay. Before our family gathered at the dinner table, my brother and I sat at the window, our eyes glued to the darkening sky to wait for the first star which would herald the start of our Christmas celebrations.

When we saw it we shouted, "Here's the first star!"

Janusz and I as small children

Emelia, Janusz and I

Me as a young girl

My first communion

Renia and I, First Communion, June 1939

The Christmas candles were lit on the tree and the feast began. Of course we don't have candles now in Africa because of fires, but there we could. We had special bread, *oplatek*, in the shape of little squares. Each had a beautiful scene pressed into it. The bread was similar to communion wafers. The wafers were usually handed out by the father of the house. Each member of the family was given a piece of wafer which they, in turn, presented to a loved one who ate it. After eating the wafers, they wished each other a happy Christmas and happiness and health for the New Year. After *Mamusia* (mum) and *Tatus* (dad) had broken the bread we all started to eat.

There were twelve meatless dishes. These represented the twelve apostles. The dishes were mostly fish such as jellied eel and herring. There were also vegetables and all this was followed by plum pudding. After dinner we sang carols and opened presents with all the excitement children experience. At about half past eleven we all climbed into sleighs and rode to church for Christmas midnight mass, the ringing of the sleigh bells echoing the sound of the church bells which we could hear all around us. It was all so different, so beautiful. I never talk about it now and try not to think about it.

When we got home after church we sat around and had cake and tea. We talked animatedly into the early hours of the morning. I recall all the joy and happiness of a close-knit family.

We did not go to church on Christmas morning. We woke up around 11am and enjoyed a traditional meal of ham and other goodies.

Another important aspect in my childhood memories is the close friend who lived nearby. She was Renia Gora. We spent a lot of time together. This friendship would stand the test of time.

The journey from paradise to purgatory

Our wonderful life was destined not to last. There was talk of unrest and of Germans occupying Poland. As a child I don't remember much of this 'pre-war' talk. What was actually happening was the invasion of western Poland by the German army. The punitive treaty of Versailles, which had been signed at the end of World War I, was between the victorious western Allies and, under protest, the German leaders. It was an attempt to prevent any future German invasions. It was, however, not worth the paper on which it was written.

In 1933 Hitler was made chancellor of Germany. To the Allied countries, exhausted after the war, he seemed to be trying to restore German pride. The Allies, reluctant to contemplate another war, did not interfere in Hitler's creating his *Lebensraum* (living space). He re-armed the Rhineland in 1936, however, and took over much of German-speaking Czechoslovakia in 1938. In 1939 he annexed the rest of Czechoslovakia.

As early as 1938 Stalin had become suspicious of Hitler's ambitions. However, Soviet attempts at getting British and French cooperation against Nazi Germany were unsuccessful. Fearing what could end up as a futile lone war against the German army, Stalin agreed to the non-aggression pact offered by Hitler.

On 23 August 1939 the agreement was signed, with Eastern Europe divided into sections. Poland was to be partitioned. One of the benefits this pact offered the German army was that they were now able to concentrate on one war front at a time. As far as the Soviets were concerned, it meant that they were diverting German attention away from the USSR which allowed them to build up their own defenses. The Germans invaded Poland from its western borders on 1 September 1939. The Polish army was no match for the well-equipped Germans, and they were defeated in a matter of weeks. On 17 September of the same year the USSR attacked Poland from the east.

At this time I could sense the concern of my parents, but I only realised that there was trouble when they told me that if I heard sirens I should go to the cellar because there could be bombing. My first bad experience was when Janusz and I were walking in town and the sirens went off and a woman grabbed us and took us into a cellar. I was too young to understand the politics or what was really happening. I only knew that my part of Poland was occupied by the Russians. I also knew that my 16-year-old cousin, Stach Gawronski, had been killed after he joined the Polish underground movement.

Up to that time I had not known any hardship. The worst thing that had happened to me was having measles and the time when Janusz contracted diphtheria and I had to throw sweets to him through the window because I was not allowed to go near him for fear of catching the disease.

Then we heard the bad news that the Russians and the Germans had formed an alliance – something particularly daunting as the Germans were occupying the western part of Poland and the Russians the east. I remember the Russian tanks rumbling through town. My parents were very worried but, being a child, I was not too concerned about the bigger picture of what was happening in the war. My world was my home, my family and my friends. I had been brought up with strong values of what was right and wrong and the attitude of many Poles, especially those living in our town, was an enigma. I couldn't understand why some of them welcomed the Russians with garlands of flowers and led them into the town waving red flags. People seemed to be so fickle. They changed according to the way the wind blew. This was a trend that I was to see repeated in later years.

My father and all other local officials had to leave town and flee to Lithuania for safety. It was no longer safe to live in a big house. Communists despised capitalism and saw it as something to be punished, so we were unsafe in our beautiful home and Tatus was able to smuggle us out of our house before he could be

My father (second from left) in his official regalia

arrested by the Militia which had been formed by local Soviet sympathisers. He found a place for us to stay in a humble cottage on the outskirts of the town. He then fled into hiding to better protect us.

Russians were everywhere. The officers would come into a house and ask how many rooms there were, and if you had two bedrooms and a lounge they would say, "We will leave one room for you." They did not believe that a family needed a whole cottage to itself, so they commandeered all the rooms and housed various Soviet soldiers there. We were not spared. Mother, Janusz and I had to suffer the humiliation of living in one room. When Father later returned and joined us he also had to share this sparse accommodation.

We were very lucky. God looked after us throughout my life. The Russian officer in our house was a very nice man. Most of the Russians were of peasant stock and very different from our family but this officer was kind. He gave us sweets. He even brought little gifts of food when ours was in short supply. Mother was able to speak Russian as a result of her experiences during World War I – and her first time in Siberia – so there was communication.

At first the Soviet NKVD seemed to adopt a friendly attitude towards the local people. They spent their rubles in the shops and seemed to be trying to win over our people. Children were able to attend schools. Churches remained open (this was a shrewd move by the Soviets as there would have been an outcry had they closed them) but the Madonna and child that had always hung in our classroom was replaced by pictures of Lenin and Stalin. We also noticed that some of our classmates were missing from their seats. People in high places were being de-ported to Siberia. Men who were civic, religious or business leaders disappeared. These were people who, with their leadership ability to move a crowd, were a threat as they could inspire resistance among our people. No one knew anything about them and thought they would never be seen again. I was only nine years old and I found this time to be sad and confusing. My father fled and I felt very insecure. I did not understand all the implications of what was happening. After some time Father did return to the cottage and stayed there in hiding for a while. This was after the Russians had taken over Lithuania and he was again forced to flee.

One day in February one of the officers informed my mother that the militia were searching for my father and that if they found him his fate would be un-known. Polish intelligentsia who were found were shot or thrown into jail and not heard from again. I just remember Father putting on his coat. I remember the colour of it – black. He took his hat and his little suitcase and walked across the border into the part of Poland under German occupation, and out of our lives for 18 years.

On 13 April, in the early hours of the morning, I was awakened by a noise coming from our neighbour's house. Our nanny, Emilia, went to investigate.

Renia and her family had moved into this house. Renia later told me how the militia, armed with bayonets, knocked at the door and told them they were to be taken to a place of safety. Fortunately, Renia's father, an important man in the Polish police, had already fled. My mother and Emilia heard the commotion and went to the assistance of our friends. Emilia came back to our house to make them cocoa. The militia, however, had other ideas and prevented Renia, her brother and her mother from leaving the house by putting bayonets to their backs and pushing them back into the house. The militia asked Renia's mother if she knew where Mrs Kuchcinska lived, little knowing that my mother was actually in the house helping with the packing.

Later, I watched as the family was loaded onto sleighs. I didn't know they were searching for us. My peace of mind was short-lived. As soon as the militia realised who we were they instructed us to also pack as we too were to be taken to this 'place of safety'. The militia raided the house and took everything of value. When other officers were out of earshot, one kind Russian soldier urged Mother to pack warm clothes and to take the family photo album. When the other soldiers were close he, too, shouted, "Hurry up! Hurry up!" I picked up my doll but found little comfort and no warmth in my heart for even the kindest soldier. My hatred was intense. These people, who had taken away my lovely home and sent Father into exile, were now depriving us of everything else.

We were taken to the railway station where we met up with Renia and her family. We saw hundreds and hundreds of people – many whose faces we knew – women, children and old men. It was chaos – dark and cold. After waiting on the platform for some time, we heard the whistle of the freight train that sounded like a cry of agony. We were unceremoniously herded into the boxcars which were usually used for transporting cattle. The trucks were spartan with bars at the windows and plank floors. There was no bedding. We had to sleep on the planks. There were so many people in those trucks. After we had been pushed into the trucks, the doors were slammed behind us and we were plunged into near darkness, the only light coming from the slits between the planks of the walls of the boxcar and from the small, barred windows. This was a huge train and we were packed in like sardines. There were no toilets and we had to make use of the gaps in the uneven planks. When I wanted to lie down I had to slide down from the top to get a little space. To make matters worse, Mother had an ear infection and was not well. She was not the only one feeling the strain. People were crying and being sick. There was so much misery. The nightmare journey lasted for nearly a month.

We did not know where the train was taking us. We seemed to be travelling though the whole of eastern Europe. My friend Renia recognised the unimpressive Ural mountains when we crossed them. They brought us very salty soup, laced with lots of pepper, with chunks of heavy bread. Sometimes the train would stop at a siding in the early hours of the morning and I would trade things, like my hair ribbons, for a little tin of water to stop the thirst caused by the soup. The Russians we saw at these sidings also seemed hungry. I saw some of them digging for food in rubbish bins. They seemed to be oppressed, battling to survive.

Renia felt that we were more fortunate than most because her nanny had given her family a sack of dried bread. Her family lived for months with the fear of deportation because of other deportations that had occurred on 10 February and they knew that they too were in danger. Because of this they were more prepared. The dried bread turned out to be very useful. The Soviets sometimes gave us hot water called kibatok in which we dipped the bread.

Only twice during this long journey were we allowed to use the toilets at the sidings. Otherwise we were told to relieve ourselves under the trucks on adjacent railway lines. Renia has the horrific recollection of the trucks moving while a small boy of about six years was under it relieving himself. She still remembers the screams of the mother as the boy was crushed by the wheels of the moving truck.

Thinking back over this terrible time Renia said, "Humans are very cruel and they will never learn. Cruelty is still going on all over the world. Hitler gassed so many millions of Jews and Poles. Millions of people perished in the Russian takeover and now people are perishing everywhere all over the world. Can we ever change?"

On one occasion when the train stopped I remember having to step over dead bodies lying in the road. Starvation was rife throughout the land. Hunger not only affected the prisoners of war. Other causes of death were far too ghastly to contemplate. Walking over dead bodies was not easy for me. Mother took my hand and said, "Just walk." With legs that felt like wooden logs, I did as I was told.

Janusz only remembers one incident from our journey to hell. He recalls that we had to get off the train in order to shower. He thinks that we were to be disinfected. We all had to take off our clothes. There was no respect for human decency – men and women all had to strip out in the open. Cramped between naked bodies, Janusz, who was only six years old, looked up and saw a naked woman standing next to him. It was the first time that he had seen a woman without clothes. The mischievous Janusz told me that he found this to be quite an exciting experience – perhaps a hint of what was to happen in the future?

Life in Siberia

The train passed through what seemed like an eternity of sky and space. We crossed over slow rivers twisting themselves like venomous snakes and chugged over the Siberian plains. Siberia seemed to be an immense spread of bleak plains which, from our cramped viewpoint, looked very ominous. We also thought about the fate of the Czar Nicholas and his family who had been butchered at Yekaterinburg. How far away from this dreadful place were we? What was our fate? Would we fare as badly as the previous group of Poles?

Finally, we reached our destination. We were unloaded at bayonet point onto a station about 30km from a small village in northern Kazakstan. We were then transported in trucks to the village and unceremoniously deposited in the middle of a square with our suitcases and belongings. We were herded into a big building which could have been some sort of recreational club. We were told that we had to find our own accommodation in the village. We trudged out onto a road shining with black mud and puddles.

The houses in the village were small and poor. Mostly they were a bare wooden shell with cow dung on the floors for warmth. Some of these humble dwellings offered only one room where the family slept, and – if lucky – perhaps a small kitchen. Like all the other women, Mother struggled through the mud and slush, knocking on village doors, begging for a place to stay. The Russian people were hostile towards us because they had been told that we were their enemies. We, the Polish people, were labeled as rich and guilty of oppressing those who had nothing. Later, once we began talking with one another, the local attitudes began to change.

One peasant family on whose door Mother knocked said that they were willing to share their simple accommodation if we did not mind sleeping on the floor in the same room as them. We moved in with this family where we spent the next few days. Our battle with fleas and lice began here.

Eventually, Renia's mother found a small, empty shack outside the collective farm so we agreed to move in together. In fact, four families – mothers and seven children – moved in.

The house offered no luxuries or even simple amenities. There was one big room with a little stove in the centre and another, smaller room. Four women and their children worked hard to make the cottage habitable. Three families slept on planks of wood raised up from the mud floor in the main room, where we also cooked our food. The other family slept in the small room. We lived there for about a month.

While living in this shack we had to collect our own firewood. We did not have permission to do this so we were, in fact, stealing it. After each search for firewood, we returned to the hut scratching ourselves, covered with red blotches. While we were in the woods collecting branches for our fire we would be attacked by millions of mosquitoes. It was most unpleasant and we always had to run for cover, but not before we had been thoroughly bitten. Neither Mother ('Mrs Judge') nor Renia's mom ('Mrs Policeman') had any experience of chopping wood. Once, while trying to chop wood with an axe, one of the mothers nearly cut off her foot. Fortunately Renia's mother knew a little first aid and bandaged the foot which healed remarkably well.

Life there was not all bad. We explored the woods, invented our own games and even played 'Cowboys and Indians'. We also played a sort of modified American baseball. As children, we were blissfully unaware of the real dangers and hardships. I suppose this was because we were so sheltered by our mothers. Janusz even thought this time to be an adventure. When it was too cold to play outside he found it frustrating to have to remain in the crowded, small wooden house.

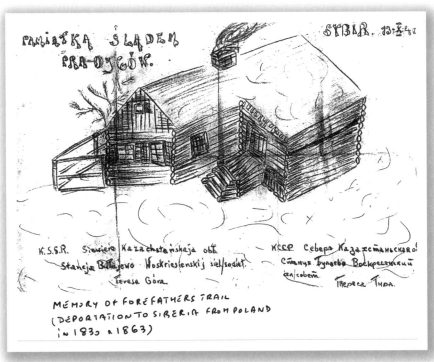

A sketch of the Siberian house as Renia remembered it

The Polish deportees met in the evenings to pray together. We prayed for the ability to survive the hardships of Siberia and to return home. The Polish children had to attend a Russian school; most of us could not speak Russian, but we learned it very quickly – and some of us even ended up at the top of our class. One Christmas we organised a play at the school and performed a Polish dance for our classmates.

It was a continuous fight for survival against totalitarian Soviet oppression. Our mothers were strengthened by their faith in God and their patriotism. All the children were forced to attend Russian schools where we were exposed to indoctrination and atheism.

Janusz remembers the school we attended. He recalls one of the school books had a picture of Stalin on the cover. He drew pictures all over Stalin's face, totally disfiguring it. The teacher saw it and Janusz got the biggest hiding of his life. It was the first time he had been beaten with a cane. I still believe that it was thanks to God that the episode ended with a caning. Sometimes children and their parents disappeared never to be seen again after similar incidents.

There were many Russian people living in the village who were far less fortunate than us. Behind the village there was a little mud hut where a Jewish family lived. There were about five children in this family and they had absolutely nothing. The Polish families felt they had more than this poor family and so we shared whatever we could. We managed to give them odd scraps of bread for which they were very grateful.

We did not always have enough to eat ourselves and we often went to bed hungry. But we were better off than the women and children who were among the first to be deported from Poland. These people were taken to the very northern part of Russia to a remote forest called Tajga in Siberia. Here they were set to work cutting wood. They were completely cut off from the rest of the world. Each day they received about five hundred grams of Russian bread – no fruit or vegetables. Many developed scurvy. Many died. The ones who lived cared for the orphans so that they did not have to go to Russian orphanages as these had a dreadful reputation.

Each morning, while we lived in the village the women had to report for work at the Kolchoz – this was the Russian collective farm. They were forced to till the earth which had been frozen to stone by the cold winters. It was at the Kolchoz that they were given food – usually a piece of bread or a flask of milk. This was the payment for their labours. Mother was able to bring a little food home for us. There was never enough food for our families, so we were forced to barter with the local peasants. We would exchange a sheet or blouse or some beads for bread, potatoes or flasks of milk. Occasionally mother was able to bring home a dish that was the Russian staple food. It consisted of burnt bacon, salted fat and bread

Russian school – I am in the second row from the top, second from left

which they dipped into the meat dish. It was awful, full of fat and greasy, but we were so hungry that even this was eaten with relish.

It was significant that the poor people of Poland had not been deported – only the families of the educated, wealthy and important, people with degrees such as police officers, members of the military, teachers, professors, religious leaders and their families. The communist idea was that, without these people, they could destroy Polish heritage. Many of the men that they took were shot or put into prisons and never seen again. In Katin about 20 000 Polish officers and policemen were shot and buried in one mass grave. There was an investigation after the war and the Russians blamed the Germans, but there was no doubt that Germans would not do that on Russian soil. The atrocity was perpetrated by the Soviet NKVD. This was later confirmed by the Russians. We were not watched or guarded in the village. But we still felt like prisoners. Escape was impossible. There was nowhere to go. If one of us were to try to escape it would end in death – either from starvation and freezing in the deep snow or from a bullet in the back.

One day there was a fire in the chimney of our shack. Many people came to our assistance with buckets of water mostly because they were afraid that the fire would spread and endanger the village. The authorities deemed the shack unsafe to live in as a serious fire would inevitably spread, so we had to look for other accommodation. At this point the families split up, each finding a small corner in a peasant's house. In the cottage in which we found accommodation we slept on pallets next to the fire. Behind our sleeping place was an opening where the cattle and sheep were kept. In winter the livestock helped to warm the humble dwelling.

The following spring the Russians came and rounded up all the women who had two children or fewer. We were to be transported to another place because we were going to be 'privileged' to help to build Russia. We were not given any choice. We were prisoners even though we were not behind bars. Once again we were herded into cattle trucks and taken to another part of Kazakstan in Russia. Our 'privilege' was to build a railway line between two villages. Mother and the other women were put to work laying the tracks. They also had to build three barracks along the railway line in which we could live. These were little more than wooden shacks with planks for beds, lined up in rows against the walls. There were 20 to 30 people allocated to each barrack. Every day a mother was left in the barrack to care for the children. The rest were marched out to work. Every few weeks we had to move the barracks, slowly progressing through the countryside as one section of the track was completed and the next began.

After a while my mother and some of the other women were moved to another camp where we had to live in tents. We were separated from our friends Renia and her family, who remained in the barracks from which they were eventually rescued. I did not know why we were being moved. Perhaps it was part of a psychological disorientation programme on the part of the Russian authorities – not wanting the deportees to feel too settled. In this new camp there were only ten toilet facilities for all of us – hundreds of us. There was only one fireplace for warmth or cooking. It had to be shared with about thirty other people. We were starving: imagine 15 or 20 families trying to cook a meal on one little stove! We had to queue. I remember the cruelty of people. I recall trying to cook, putting my little pot with flour or water on the fire and being pushed aside by adults. On the other hand, if someone was sick or if anybody died, there was always help.

We had to do our share of work to maintain life. We were responsible for furtively collecting firewood and standing in queues to try to get Russian bread or stealing salt from the salt trucks. I used to get up very early in the morning, about 4am, to stand in the queue in an attempt to be near the front. I would meekly stand in the queue to await my turn. Janusz would wake up late and return early; I would only get home after dark. His secret was that he always looked for an old lady with a kind face. He would tell her that his mother had stood there. The people at the back of the queue would begin screaming, but the old lady would always seem to let him in. I found this annoying, but even at that early age Janusz had heaps of charm and was a beautiful child. Sometimes I felt that I could strangle him, but my love for him never faded.

It was unbelievably cold and the tents offered little warmth. The women tried to do everything in their power to improve the situation. This was when they cut turf – not the lovely green clumps of grass we know, but rather sodden brown pieces of earth where grass may once have tried to grow – and they placed these clods of earth on the outside surfaces of the tents to act as insulation. The canvas was slippery and the clods kept slipping off, but the women persevered. It was a brave attempt to keep the tents warm.

We had a never-ending struggle for survival. In summer one of the main crops on the state farms was sunflowers. They were grown for their seeds, a great favourite of the Russian people. They would toss them into their mouths and spit out the pips. Janusz and I crept into the fields and stole as many sunflower seeds as we could. Stealing was obviously very dangerous. Had we been caught the punishment would have been severe – a beating or worse. We cleaned the seeds and sold them to passengers when trains stopped at the railway sidings, keeping alert for officials. Sometimes the trains would not stop so we ran alongside the slow moving trains shouting, 'A ruble a glass, a ruble a glass!' With the few Russian rubles we were able to go to the canteen and bought some miserable cabbage soup. Janusz remembers that he was very good at stealing. He feels that this was the start of his bad ways. He thinks that the actual skill he learned was not theft but survival. We had to steal in order to survive. Being a little older I still knew that what we were doing was wrong, but stealing was acceptable among us during that time in Siberia. As the children of a judge in Swieciany it would never have been right. Janusz was much younger and he was still learning about what was right and what was wrong. Years later as a young teenager, Janusz could not conceptualise that stealing was bad because, as a small boy, he had been praised for it.

In the Siberian camps I became *Mamusia* (Mother) and teacher to my brother Janusz. I had to do this because Mother was often away from us working on the railway lines. Janusz once said that I was very mature at this young age. A few years his senior but very wise. I felt that it was my duty to care for my little brother. I feel that this role has never ended. In Siberia my childhood was taken away from me. I was forced into an adult situation. Sometimes I was a person that I did not like very much.

Our small contribution from the sale of sunflower seeds helped the pauper income earned by Mother. In a communist regime everybody works for the state and she was forced to work on the railway lines. It was hard, physical work, moving stones and putting them under the railway tracks. The women were called out at all hours of the night to unload trucks, or break the rails in winter and support them with gravel. Mother would return home late at night, or in the early hours of morning, exhausted, her hands frozen with frostbite. She would hide a little bread or whatever else she had been given as rations, under her cloak to share with us. We were always hungry. I remember that once when we were unbearably hungry

Janusz and I planned how we could catch and kill a dog belonging to one of the camp officials. Fortunately we were unsuccessful.

With the other things we had brought with us we had one of Father's suits hoping that we would see him again. We did not sell Father's suit at this time, but it was to prove very useful at a later stage. The local people probably benefited from the exchanges we made with them because they acquired good things that they would otherwise never have possessed. They were simple people, who had never been far from this village. They were born there, married there and died there, never having seen the beauty or sophistication of places like St Petersburg or other beautiful places in the world. It was sad.

A bright spot in this grey and white existence were the food parcels that were sent to us by our *Tatus* (Father). Emilia, our nanny, would cross the border from Poland's Russian zone and go to the German zone in order to get the parcels sent to us. She got our address from the Red Cross. Father was also able to send medicine when Janusz had pneumonia. Father communicated with us under the name of a friend of my mother's. He wrote to us as a woman.

I had a trunk. I don't remember where I got it from. It could have come with us from Poland or I may have found it in the house we first lived in, I don't know, but it was very useful for storing food, especially the treats Emilia sent. I was in charge of the food. One day I found that Janusz had raided the trunk and eaten everything in it. I was very angry. Janusz did not seem to worry too much about my anger probably because his tummy was full for the first time in a long while. After this I kept the trunk locked. I found myself hoarding food and medicines for the months when I thought there would be nothing. I had a sense of survival even though I was young. Janusz used to say, "Come, let's eat this today." But I kept it locked. If anything was in supply in the village, I used to get it and lock it away. I had quite a lot and I'm sure this saved our lives.

Mother was a devout Christian all her life. For us, at that time, our religion must have been quite shallow. We followed the beliefs of Mother with childlike trust. We believed in God because we were told to. I had many questions about God: where was He when He was so desperately needed? Were we being punished by Him for sins we had committed? Was He so ashamed of the wickedness of the world that He had forsaken us?

I used to cry often. I tried to control my emotions by telling myself that tears would not help. I prayed because my parents had taught me to pray and it seemed the right thing to do. But I couldn't see God or even any evidence that there was a God. I had so many questions but few answers. My biggest question was whether or not I would ever see *Tatus* again. Although we did receive letters and parcels from him, my doubts were ever present. I felt it was a hopeless situation. But Mother's faith was strong and this strength kept our family together. Mother would say, "Don't worry. Things are going to come right. Have faith. You are going to see Father again. There will be an end to this because there is God."

This was not an easy time for Christians in Russia. I remember having a little cross torn from my neck by the teacher in the school. People in Russia were not allowed to talk about God. If they dared talk about religion they were punished. However, worship still happened in secret. In one house we visited we were shown an icon of the Madonna concealed behind the red flag. Communism was oppressive. Not only did we suffer, but the local peasants also suffered, as did many other Russians. They had little food; families were separated; there was no trust within families, and brother was frightened of brother. Even things said within the confines of a family gathering were reported back to the government and people were arrested. The only Russians who seemed to benefit from the Communist regime were the officials.

Poor diet and unhealthy living conditions began taking their toll. I developed problems with my teeth. My baby teeth wouldn't fall out naturally while my permanent teeth began growing. I was in considerable pain and started running a fever. Mother heard about someone in the next village who helped with pulling teeth. Actually he was a butcher by trade. This village was about fifteen miles away. Before leaving for the dentist we had to report to the camp authorities in order to get permission to leave our village. To reach the dentist we had to walk through a forest. I was running a temperature and needed lots of encouragement along the way. Mother promised that she would buy me sugar once we had reached the village. This was a huge incentive as I had neither seen nor tasted sugar for ages.

What the butcher's qualifications were in the skill of dentistry was unknown but, because there were no hospitals or properly trained doctors, people were forced to make use of his services. There were no anaesthetics or injections, and the process of tooth-pulling was excruciatingly painful. I was unable to suppress my screams.

The butcher did not enjoy this lack of appreciation for his handy-work. "You had better stop your fussing, young lady," he said, "If you don't I will not attend to your teeth."

There was nothing that I would have liked more.

"It hurts so much." I said, distraught, "I don't mind if you don't fix my teeth."

"Come, come now Alutka darling," said Mother, very close to tears herself. "If you are a good girl and stop crying then this kind man can attend to your teeth, and I will buy you some beautiful things."

The butcher extracted six milk teeth.

I don't remember getting the promised sugar or the beautiful things, probably because there wasn't anything to buy in the shops. The return journey, walking through the dark forest, past wolves and heaven only knew what other nasty things, was horrendous. The sombre branches of birch and conifer seemed to reach out to clutch at my clothes.

Even in this desolation there were still small miracles. One day we saw a man walking down the road towards our tents. He was wearing a uniform we didn't recognise. Curiosity brought everyone out of their tents to see what was happening. The man must have been some kind of Polish soldier. He was actually looking for my mother's friend.

When he spoke it was with the voice of an angel. "There is an end to it," he said. "Your friend's husband is out of prison and I have come to take them to him in the south of Russia. The allied forces and the Russians have joined together to fight against the Germans. Russia is releasing all the prisoners and there is going to be a war between Russia and Germany. There's hope for all of us."

Isolated as we had been in our remote Siberian village we did not know all the events of the war that had led up to our saviour arriving in our compound. In spite of warnings to the contrary, Stalin, in his arrogance, was convinced that Germany would not attack the USSR. The badly equipped Soviet army stationed along the western front was ordered to avoid 'provocation'. The result was that it had no chance against the efficient Germans when they attacked. The Soviets suffered terrible losses. But the Red army was not to be denied. By December 1941 it had built up its reserves. Blood was spilt on both sides in the many battles for supremacy. After the German invasion of the USSR Britain offered the Soviets help. An agreement was signed on the 12 July 1941. The Americans also offered support after Hitler declared war on the US in December 1941.

One of the best recorded battles was the isolation of the German forces in their attempt to conquer Stalingrad. Their defeat was announced on Moscow radio in February 1943. Soviet domination over Germany was completed by May 1945. By this time they had invaded much of eastern Europe including Poland. This, however, was long after we were safely out of Russia.

The Polish sergeant who had miraculously appeared in our Siberian camp recognised Mother and urged her to try to raise some money so that she could pay for our train fare while there was the chance or we might never be able to leave Siberia. We would go to the south of Russia to join the Polish army. Mother, in her goodness, regretted the thought of leaving the friends she had made at the camp. She felt that she was deserting them.

I was determined that we would leave. Armed with Father's suit and the few things still left in the suitcase for bartering, I walked to a nearby Mongol village. I was alone and very frightened, but I sold the suit for six hundred rubles and a bag of flour. I was successful in getting enough money for our train fare. We boarded a goods train with other families and left Siberia forever.

The town we travelled to was in Uzbekistan. We were welcomed by the Polish army. It was wonderful. We were clothed and fed and, best of all, we were with the Polish army, people from our own country. A Polish general, General Anders, was in charge. This was a relief as our trust in the Russians was at a low ebb. The general approached the British and the Americans in an attempt to get them to move the Polish refugees away from Soviet soil because of our distrust of the communists. I don't remember how long we stayed in this camp, but I do remember soldiers making an army uniform for Janusz of which he was inordinately proud.

Finally the order came for the Polish unit to leave Russia. We went with them. We were taken in army trucks and boarded boats to cross the Caspian Sea. There were huge storms once we were out at sea. It was a terrible journey. The ship was overcrowded and most of the travellers were horribly seasick. We had to sleep in one of the lifeboats and were terribly cold. By this time our suitcases were empty and all we had left to cover ourselves were a few sheets. People were dying of dysentery and typhus. Going to the toilet on the ship was a nightmare. The queues were endless. There was no water. The hellish journey lasted two days.

Tehran

At the end of the voyage we were unceremoniously dumped on a beach and then had to endure a delousing programme. We were given food and transported in lorries to Tehran. I think we were taken to Tehran and not back to Poland because travel in Eastern Europe would have been too difficult as battles were still raging between the German and Red armies. It was another terrible journey. The terrain was very mountainous; one of the trucks flipped over and many people were killed.

The food, weather and our general living conditions in Tehran were such that life was very difficult. The weather seemed to go from one extreme to another – either freezing cold or boiling hot. As I remember, the school we attended was held on an old runway of some sort. We sat on stones and it was extremely hot. There were no buildings or shelter and we didn't have hats to protect us from the sun. We had come from the icy cold of Siberia and our bodies couldn't take the heat. I ended up with sunstroke, as did many others.

Janusz was still a little boy. His zest for life could not be easily quelled for long. I had been forced to grow up prematurely, yet I too craved childlike pastimes. We explored as much of Tehran as we could and even found some exciting underground passages.

The food was foreign to us and our already sensitive stomachs rebelled. We were also susceptible to other illnesses. Huge tents were erected on the opposite side of Tehran to serve as a field hospital, but these were totally inadequate. The number of graves of Polish people in Tehran is enormous – absolutely enormous – so many people died.

The unsanitary conditions in which we lived at the army barracks, not having soap or hot water for washing, primitive toilets and lice were conducive to the spread of disease. I remember my mother working hard, trying to save my beautiful long blonde hair when I had lice. One horrifying day both my mother and my brother got very, very ill. We called for an ambulance. Because the hospital tents were on the other side of Tehran, I didn't receive news of either my mother or brother. I remember being very distressed. I must have been around 12-years-old. I will never forget this time. There wasn't sympathy from other women in the camp. I was still made to take my turn carrying the big bucket of hot soup, even though my family was not there. I suppose everyone has a breaking point and this was mine. The deprivation and hardship we had been through had been awful, but I had always had my family with me and now that comfort had been taken away. I was gripped by emotion beyond my understanding.

The indignities and suffering of captivity made people brutal and unfeeling. The experiences of one woman in the camp made her immune to my pain. She told me to stop moping around, adding, "Get up on your feet. Just accept that your mother and brother are dead and start your life all over again. Crying is not going to help you."

Shortly after this we had to move camp. Space on the lorries was in short supply. I was alone with no adult to champion my cause and had to fight for my right to travel with my small bundle of possessions. I was a child and the stronger, older women threw my luggage off the truck. Finally I succeeded in getting a space. We were moved to another tented camp.

Throughout my life there have been miracles and the timing of the latest one could not be more perfect. One day I heard my name called. This was an incredible moment in my life.

There was this man standing in the tent opening and he said, "I'm a doctor. I used to play bridge with your mother and father in Poland. I've seen your mother. She had typhus badly and it manifested itself twice. Your brother had very, very bad dysentery. But they are now both alive and on their way to getting better."

I badly wanted to see my mother, but it was dangerous for a blonde girl to be alone in Tehran. People used to kidnap girls who were fair as there was a great demand for them in the local brothels. The kind doctor paid a woman to take me to see my mother. I covered my hair with a scarf and climbed onto a bus. My mother said that if it had not been for the doctor she would not have lived. But she indeed survived and came back to the camp. She immediately went to work in order to augment our income.

Janusz looks back: "I remember being sent to the tent hospital. I was nine and it was my first near-death experience. I had lapsed into a coma and was pronounced dead. As there was a massive shortage of beds at the hospital, my body was unceremoniously piled into a donkey cart and take to a nearby graveyard to join the hundreds of other corpses. The gravedigger picked me up and was about to toss me into a grave when I suddenly opened my eyes. I don't know who got the bigger fright – him or me – but he was certainly the ugliest one-eyed man I'd ever seen in my life, but a life I certainly owe to him! He hysterically mumbled something in Persian or Arabic before dumping me back on the narrow donkey cart to take me back to the tent hospital. My mother was frantic as she had absolutely no idea what had become of me."

The wheels of history, however, were turning and the time had come for us to leave Tehran. Refugees were to be taken to many different lands and the costs were covered by the Polish Government in London. Food shortages in the country had resulted in riots. Revolutionaries had broken into the palace of the Shah of Persia and authorities were worried about the safety of the refugees in the camps. For ten nights we mounted a vigil in the fear of an attack, but finally we were evacuated and we boarded a ship bound for Africa. The ship was commissioned to carry Polish orphans to South Africa, but the passenger list included many refugees in its cargo. My mother was employed as a nurse for the duration of the voyage. We were lucky enough to travel first class and received all the attention that first class passengers might expect. We had luxury accommodation, stewards to make up our beds and bring us sweets, and we dined in the first class dining room with the officers. This experience had a dream-like quality after our recent hardships. We couldn't stop laughing, eating, and generally behaving as children do. We were kept away from the other passengers because of an outbreak of smallpox on the lower decks, but this didn't spoil our fun. At one time during the voyage there were severe storms. Janusz, who did not suffer sea-sickness, remembers going into the dining room and eating as much as he liked because he was the only one left standing. Eventually, we landed at Beira, Mozambique where we had to disembark. The ship continued its way south, as the hundreds of orphans were destined for *Dom Polskich Dzieci*, the Polish Children's Home, outside Oudtshoorn in the Cape. The South African government offered them refuge and many of the Polish war orphans eventually made good lives for themselves in Johannesburg, Cape Town, Durban and other cities and towns throughout South Africa.

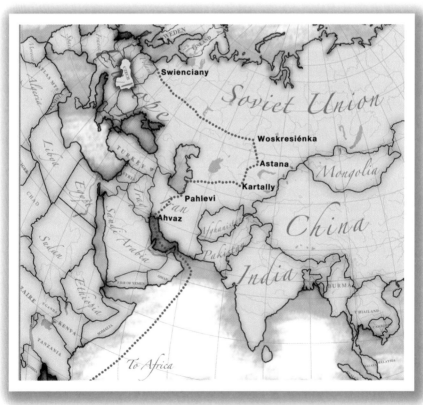

Our journey to Siberia and finally to Africa

Lusaka

We travelled from Beira to Lusaka by train. The journey took us through countryside which was so completely different from anything we had ever seen before. We were amazed by what we saw. I saw my first-ever African person working at the docks, and the truly beautiful African landscape – the bushveld. Also so much sunshine.

The Polish camp in Lusaka was outside the town. It was huge. The British had built refugee camps in Kenya, Uganda, Tanganyika, Northern and Southern Rhodesia. Hundreds of people were moved to the camp in Lusaka. My family was allocated a square, one-roomed bungalow. There were now four of us as Mother had adopted a little girl, Lucia, who had lost her parents. Fortunately she was later reunited with her mother.

The camp was jointly managed by a British commander and a Polish commandant. Mother got a job as private secretary to the Polish commandant. Although she had never received formal training, the work experience she had gained in Tehran stood her in good stead. Her salary was about six pounds a month which, added to the ten shillings allowance, was very important to us. All children received two shillings and sixpence a month pocket money. In those days it was a lot of money. Once a month we were able to go to the cinema in Lusaka. We had to walk six miles to the town, and the movies cost us six pence, but what a treat. Weekdays we attended the camp's Polish school.

Once again we were hungry. The good food we had eaten on the ship from Tehran sharpened our disappointment with the poor camp fare. It was a shock that very first morning when we went to collect our food from the canteen. We were given brown bread with marmalade. This was bad for us because we never had marmalade in Poland – it was bitter. We always had sweet jam. At lunch time there would be mielie pap and a bit of stew or a bit of sauce or something and occasionally we had pierogi, a special Polish dish which is pastry filled with minced meat – and that was when Janusz and I had fist fights over the food! I'm not proud of this. It was sad. Perhaps these fights were indicative of the desperation we experienced even in this kinder environment.

The Lusaka camp did offer security and assured meals even if the food was insufficient and strange. There was no communism, suspicion or mistrust. We had a lot of fun there. We made friends with the other children and played games such as volleyball by making our own net from a piece of rope. Someone also found an old gramophone and a squeaky record. Some evenings we would come together to sing and dance. It was so different to the type of fun teenagers of today enjoy; it was a simple kind of entertainment. There were no drugs or alcohol, and the

Janusz and I standing, Mother and Lucia sitting

enjoyment was total. Another treat was to go for walks outside the camp. There were no rivers nearby but we found a big fig tree. We climbed the tree and spent hours in its shade discussing matters that were important to us. I still correspond with one of the friends that I made. He now lives in France. He is a retired engineer, but in the camp he used to help me with my maths. I always struggled with maths.

My teacher at the Polish camp school doubted my future success in life because of my lack of maths skills. We really didn't see eye to eye. I still think my failure in maths was partly because I didn't like the teacher. Other teachers tried to support me, saying, "She's so good in all her other subjects. She should not fail just because of one subject."

But his response was, "She will not do well in life, so why bother to pass her if she has no knowledge of maths?"

Surprisingly today I use maths most efficiently in my work as well as when I play bridge.

The school was overcrowded, but there was no proper high school at that time. We had to write an entrance examination in order to attend a high school outside

Josef Milewski, who helped me with my maths, Lucia and I

Displaced family: Janusz, Mother and I outside our hut

Marandellas in Southern Rhodesia. A school principal from Livingstone came to supervise the exam. He recognised my potential and introduced me to Dr and Mrs Rybicki, who had settled in Livingstone travelling via Cyprus. The Cyprus group were highly-educated Poles, mostly with degrees, who had fled Poland before the Russian occupation. These friends played a big role in my life. They offered me the chance to attend a Livingstone school but Mother, however, insisted I go to Diggelfold, a girls' high school outside Marandellas. I attended this school as a boarder and spent two years there.

It was a beautiful place, built among rocks. I remember this as being a good time in my life. I missed Mother and my brother, but we had good teachers and I soon made lots of new friends. In the meantime, a high school had been opened at the Polish camp in Lusaka, so I returned there to complete my matriculation. Mother then sent me to a convent outside Lusaka where I was supposed to learn to speak English, however, there were so many Polish girls there that we learned very little English. We were much more comfortable communicating in our mother tongue.

We stayed in the Lusaka camp for five years and during this time many long-lasting friendships were formed.

Life was not all good in the camp. Poverty was rife. In desperation many women turned to prostitution and that gave us a bad name. There was also diseases which further ostracized us from people living in Lusaka. I suppose we also looked strange because we did not have smart clothes and access to beauty parlours.

It came as a shock to us when we were informed that the British government was going to close all their refugee camps in Africa. They offered us a choice of going to Canada, Australia or of returning to Poland. Neither Canada nor Australia appealed to us and we were still fearful of the influence of communism in Poland. Mother would rather have died than experience the communist regime again. She did not dislike the Russian people as she had experienced a lot of kindness from many of them, but her memories of what the communists had done could not be erased. They had even taken her husband from her. She was a strong woman but everyone has their limits.

Life in Poland was still very hard for the survivors of the war. The Germans had been defeated but the freedom experienced by the people was a veneer under Russian supervision. My father was once again practicing as a judge, but he was forced to work illegally at night, advising a Polish film company in order to earn extra money to survive. Even long after the war a friend of mine, a university professor, could only afford a few bricks at a time in order to build a house. He went to Germany during his holidays to work for extra money. A once rich, thriving country had been brought to its knees. Communists had stolen

Mother and I

everything. Poland was fast becoming a communist country. To return to Poland was not an option as far as Mother was concerned.

However we needed to make plans for a life after the camp was demolished. We decided we wanted to remain in Africa. We loved the sunshine. Dr and Mrs Rybicki were now living in Livingstone and they said they would help us settle there.

The British government said that if the refugees found employment they could remain in Africa. However, the opportunities for employment were minimal mainly because most of us never really had a chance to learn English. Mrs Rybicka suggested I could go into a hospital and train as a nursing aid, or become a nanny in an English home. The thought of working in a hospital reminded me of all the misery I witnessed on the train to Siberia, as well as the things that had happened while we were living there and in Tehran, so I decided that being a nanny would be better. I was offered a position of nanny to a three-month-old baby and two other small children. I had never even changed a nappy in my life and I had no experience of handling babies or small children. The prospect was a little daunting. Mother was offered a position looking after the children of a doctor and his wife. Still, we decided to accept the posts and we moved to Livingstone.

Livingstone

I was the first to leave Lusaka. I had to travel alone in a train packed with troops. I shared the compartment with an older woman. All the troops wanted to speak to me but I could not speak English. My travelling companion loved all the attention from the guys who came to sit in our compartment but I was terribly shy, partly because I could not communicate with them. When we arrived in Livingstone I was met by my new family, Mrs and Mr Parkhurst, and my friends, Dr and Mrs Rybicki. I shudder to think what they must have thought of me when the train stopped and all these guys were there to help with my luggage.

The Parkhursts took me to see my new home, which was beautiful. My new employers were charming, but, once again, I found my lack of English created added hardship. Plus, I had to learn how to look after children and I really missed my family. It was also hard to accept that I was now a nanny. After all, as a child I had a nanny of my own, Emilia, and yet here I was a servant in someone else's house. This didn't mean that I was ungrateful for the opportunity of living in a gracious home, but when guests or friends of the family came to visit my place was in the kitchen. It was difficult.

Mother also found working as a nanny very difficult. She had good employers and when she left them they gave her a glowing reference.

While I was working for the Parkhursts I tried to improve my English. I bought newspapers and in the evenings I would sit with a paper and a dictionary, looking up all the words I didn't understand. I worked there for about a year. While there I used to take the baby out for walks in a pram. Lolly, who had come to Livingstone in 1947, noticed me wheeling the pram down the street. Maybe he was attracted by my long blonde hair. Anyway, he thought that I was the mother of the baby, so he made no attempt to get to know me.

My self-confidence took a battering while I was working as a nanny. I thought myself to be no better than a servant and I had insufficient language skills to be socially successful. I suppose that this loss of self esteem, combined with my bad experiences of food and sugar deprivation, were the cause of an eating compulsion. I would wake up at night and remember the jelly that was left over from lunch and I found this potential waste of food to be too terrible. I was unable to sleep or, if I did, I would have nightmares about the jelly left on the table. I would get up and creep to the kitchen and eat the leftovers. I started to put on weight. Through her kindness Mrs Parkhurst didn't help matters. She knew of the hardship that I had endured and she encouraged me to eat anything that I wanted. Her pity for me probably contributed to the negative results.

I did not really enjoy looking after the baby but I managed. I was, however, looking for something else to do. Dr and Mrs Rybicki's son, Leszek, worked for a newspaper, *The Livingstone Mail*. He knew beforehand what jobs were going to be advertised in the paper. One day he phoned to tell me about a position that was coming up in a restaurant-cum-bakery that was owned by the mayor. He suggested I should apply for the job. I didn't have any training in that particular field and many others applied, but I really, really wanted to work there.

I cycled down for the interview. Mrs Hewer, the manager and wife of the mayor, was interested in me, but my English was poor and she had five other applicants. She didn't think I would get the job.

"Please," I begged, "I am a very hard-working person. Give me a chance to prove myself!"

There must have been something about me that persuaded the Mayor's wife to appoint me.

The new position would pay considerably more than the five pounds a month which was my current salary. As Mother and I were still paying for Janusz's education, extra money would be very welcome. While waiting for the confirmation of my new job I house-sat for the Parkhursts while they went on holiday. On their return I joyfully told them my good news – that I got the job. They said that they were sorry to lose me, but wished me every success.

Now I had to find my own accommodation. I found a little flat and my mother moved in with me. Mother had managed to get a job as a cashier at a cinema. How wonderful it was to be together again and, with both of us earning money, we felt that things were much better.

At the bakery we served meals and sold bread and cakes. I had to familiarise myself with strange sounding names because people bought on credit. My nemesis was the Afrikaans surname 'Bezuidenhout'. I could neither spell nor pronounce it. But I was determined to succeed and spent the evenings writing and practicing the names until I mastered them. I had only been at the bakery for six months when the owner, Mrs Hewer, appointed me as her stand-in while she went on leave. I was fairly new and very young so the other employees didn't like this very much. But my honesty and hard work had paid off.

Mrs Hewer reached the age of retirement and sold the business. The new owners appointed a manager, but I found that most of the management work still fell to me. Apart from my normal duties in the bakery I was responsible for the books and the orders. The new manager enjoyed his evenings at the Zambezi Bar a little too much. The bar opened promptly at 5pm and the manager felt a burning need to celebrate the daily opening. He funded these occasions by taking money from the restaurant till which he replaced with IOU slips. These never seemed to get paid. This arrangement didn't please the owners very much – as a result, the fun-loving manager didn't last very long. On his departure I was rewarded for my hard work by being given his job – the manager's position!

It was the start of a new phase in my life. I felt that I was regaining my self-confidence and becoming an individual again. I was independent and had proved myself capable of doing something. I had risen above being a deportee, a refugee or a servant. For the first time since I had been forcibly removed from my home in Swieciany, I had my freedom. And, for the first time in many years, I didn't have to keep looking over my shoulder.

As a result of the way I was forced to spend my youth, freedom has become a real issue for me. When I give public addresses I stress how lucky South Africans are to have freedom – freedom of speech, freedom of movement, freedom of thought and freedom of action. Although the majority of South Africans experienced an oppressive regime, the modern generation simply doesn't know what it's like to live under communism where one is denied the right to express opinions – even to a close friend for fear of bugs or of being 'shopped', where life is death. In South Africa one can talk. It is a democratic country. I will never be able to sufficiently express my gratitude for that. I tell people to be grateful that they live in a country where they can speak of their ideals, where they can talk about their likes and dislikes – even of those who hold high positions in government.

At that time I did not feel comfortable about Poland. I did not think that it was totally free of communism. I felt that those in positions of authority had not experienced the horrors of a Siberian winter, and did not seem to be aware of the dangers of communism. Now things have changed a lot.

My fear of communism is still very real. Once, on a visit to Italy with my husband, I went to listen to a band playing in the park. The music was lovely, but when I saw the red flags flying and realised it was a communist rally, I burst into tears and fled from the park unable to speak and not looking where I was going. When I got back to the hotel I was still in tears. In my rush I had twisted my ankle and, because I was so upset, I had been completely unaware of the pain. As a result, I limped through England and Europe – and my holiday was ruined.

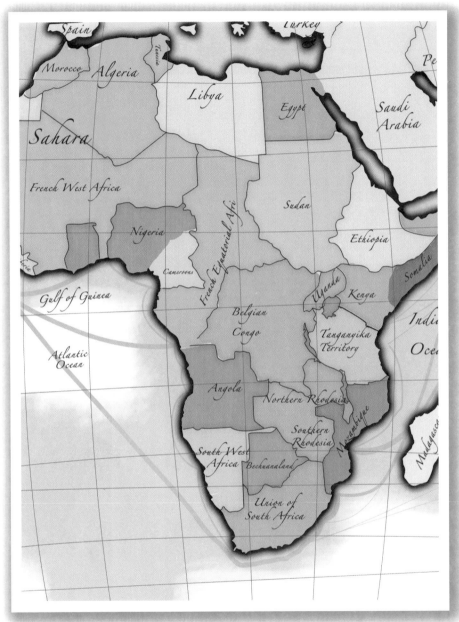

Colonial Africa circa 1940s

Ala's Story

Part 2
A New Life
1949 - 1963

Lolly

While I was working in the Livingstone bakery, Lolly came into the picture as a serious player in my life. He used to come to the café part of the bakery for his evening meal, usually accompanied by his friend Smithy with whom he shared accommodation. They were starting out in their own business and times were tough. Often they were unable to pay cash for their food, and had to give post-dated cheques. Getting money out of them was not always easy.

Up to this point I had not experienced a relationship with anyone of the opposite sex, except for Leszek (the son of Dr and Mrs Rybicki) who had found me my job at the bakery. I knew that Leszek was not really my kind of person, but I continued to be friendly with him and later with his wife over many years. He eventually died of alcohol poisoning. Although I was not aware of it, I suppose I was ready to find someone who could be a partner, and so a friendship developed between Lolly and myself.

Lolly's life had not been an easy one. His father involved himself in making of wildlife films, and often left his mother at home for great lengths of time on their farm in Skeerpoort, South Africa. His mother battled to make ends meet and even struggled to buy the children school uniforms. There were five of them altogether, four boys – Ian, Clyde, Lolly and Lesley, and one daughter, Hope. When his father returned home, he would take Lolly and his brothers out of school in order for them to do all the farming chores.

When Lolly was able to attend school he went to one in Skeerpoort. I don't think he even had a pair of shoes to wear and after school ended each day he still had to work hard on the farm. It must have been a tough childhood but probably a good grounding which established a healthy working ethos. His arrival in Livingstone happened by chance. He was on his way to work for a professor who was starting a peanut project in Tanganyika (now known as Tanzania). By the time he reached Livingstone, however, Lolly had run out of money and was not able to travel any further. He had recently broken off an engagement with another girl and was feeling sorry for himself and determined not to get involved with another woman. At that time I was 19 years old and extremely innocent. I had no conscious intention or desire of becoming entangled with a man. I wanted time to prove to myself that I was capable of getting a good job, earning a decent salary and standing on my own two feet.

One day, after I had got to know him fairly well from his visits to the café, Lolly invited me to go with him and Smithy on a rabbit hunt. I did not particularly like hunting or shooting even though my father had enjoyed the sport but now the thought of going hunting sounded exciting – or perhaps it was the prospect of spending time with this handsome young man. There I was – insecure, shy and battered by the war – accepting an invitation to do something quite daring.

On this first 'date' we drove out on the Katambora road which goes out of Livingstone. Lolly and Smithy had guns and off we went rabbit hunting, but not much hunting was done. We saw rabbits all over the place but I don't remember anyone shooting them. We had a lot of fun and there was heaps of laughter. Lolly was quite persistent and kept asking, "Why don't you ride in front with me?"

But he had another girlfriend with him – a nice, plump girl – so I said, "What about the other young lady? Don't you think she would like to be in the front with you?"

Lolly countered that by saying it was the only way in which he could teach me how to drive: "You should sit in front so that you can watch how I drive. Perhaps later you could try yourself. You won't learn if you sit in the back."

I stayed in the back, however, because I felt that it was the right place for me. When we got back home it was Smithy who kissed me goodnight.

Although I was not interested in guys at this time, I suspected that Lolly liked me simply because he had repeatedly asked me to sit in the front of the car with him.

He then invited me to go to a dance with him at the hotel. I had already accepted an invitation for the same event from the Polish guy, Leszek, so Lolly asked if I would at least have a dance with him. Boy, oh boy! It was a tango and he was a bush man – my poor toes! I knew how to dance from the parties we'd had in Lusaka with the gramophone. I loved dancing, but dancing with Lolly was a punishment. Leszek ended up in the pub (he always seemed to have a drinking problem) and left me alone so Lolly kept me company and that was the beginning of a very long association!

Lolly had arrived in Livingstone with one car and to make some money he decided to start a taxi service. When I met him things were looking up and the taxi business was flourishing. In order to expand his business, he decided to go to South Africa to buy a second car but he had no one to look after his driver in Livingstone while he was away. He asked if I would be willing to go into his office in the evenings to check that everything was alright. I agreed. While he was away his driver got drunk and smashed the car. This was a disaster but not the end of the business.

Lolly worked hard to build up his business. He shared an office with a company chartering flights over the Victoria Falls. There was a very charming lady running this venture and she tried to do Lolly's bookings as well as her employer's bookings. It didn't work too well and he suggested that I should come and work for him. I didn't think it a good proposition. I was earning fifty pounds a month at the bakery-restaurant, as well as all the food I could eat which was a good deal at that time. Plus, I was respected; people considered it to be a good job. I felt if Lolly really wanted me to work for him he would have to come up with a similar offer or I would not be interested.

At this time Lolly was staying at the Windsor Hotel which belonged to a Mrs Jordaan. He had the bright idea that if he were to buy the hotel he would be able to give me a job and any meals that I needed. Although he did not have the money he approached Mrs Jordaan and asked her if she would be willing to sell the business. When she realised who the prospective buyer was, she was concerned as to how he could afford a hotel when he hadn't even paid his rent. Her concern was very valid, but she didn't know Lolly!

He visited a nice, young Jewish man, Mr Shapiro, to borrow money for the first bond on the hotel. Mr Shapiro agreed on condition that someone else came up with the second one.

When Lolly received the money he paid the deposit on the hotel and brought his mother in to run it because she was good at catering. She had previously hired land at the Victoria Falls on the Northern Rhodesian (Zambian) side of the river where she had erected tents that she rented out during the holiday seasons, and she also prepared meals for the campers. Lolly's mom made the place quite homely and the food was very good with the result that they were kept busy. The hotel was not far from the railway station and many railway men had rooms

A float advertising our business at the Livingstone Festival

Lolly and I on the
Zambezi River

and meals there. Lolly's mom may not have been an expert financial manager, but she was a very, very hard-working lady. Her life up to this point had been a struggle because of the way her husband had neglected her. His films meant that he travelled all over the world, showing them in Australia and America, having a gorgeous time with lots of women and wild living. Once he had the bright idea of having a beach parade in Durban and selecting five of the most beautiful women for a film he planned to make while on safari. He and his son, Clyde, had great fun on the Durban beach selecting their five shapely women from about 250 applicants. The film was never made, but a marvellous time was had on safari in Mozambique with these gorgeous young ladies. They had no trouble getting through any border posts – who could resist these beauties? Clyde eventually married one of them. Lolly's father had actually made a bit of money making and selling films so he was able to really live it up. While he was travelling all over the world and going on 'safari' with beautiful women, his poor, neglected wife was left at home to look after the children.

After a few years the hotel got into financial difficulties. Lolly asked me to sort out the problem, although I had no experience in hotel management. The first thing I had to do was to stop Lolly's mom spending money and to close all the accounts. That was not easy. I needed to install a system of paying cash for everything. They owed a lot of money and paying off the debts was no easy task. Eventually, we sold he hotel.

My mother, who was still working at the cinema, was very well-known. Everyone called her 'Mrs K', and she was much loved. She was a dear, kind-hearted person. Nothing gave her greater pleasure than to buy sweets for small children who couldn't afford them.

Lolly and I started a tourism business together. We recognised the opening for tourism. We had two cars which served as taxis and he wanted to buy a launch to put on the Zambezi. He didn't have any money so he borrowed three hundred pounds from his adopted 'uncle', Ernest Glover. Ernest helped put Lolly on his feet. With the money he was able to pay the deposit on the launch. He named his business Greenway Launch and Taxi Service. At that time there was no romance at all between Lolly and I.

Lolly's first clients were a group of women from a Christian organisation who had come to visit the Victoria Falls. He had applied for permission to land on Palm Island so was able to treat these ladies to tea on the island after their trip around the other islands. It proved to be a great success.

We progressed slowly. The launch trips on the Zambezi were going smoothly and we had two taxis. We also started tours of the Victoria Falls.

Lolly decided that business and pleasure would do well together, so the romance between us began. However, it took quite a lot of persuasion for me to finally agree to getting engaged!

An introduction to wild Africa

Life was great and I was having enormous fun. It was about this time that I was invited to go on my first safari. Lolly's father was taking four Americans on a hunting trip and his sister and I were invited to join in. His mother, the chief caterer, was also included in the party. We went to the Luangwa Valley and it was a marvellous experience. Here I was – a timid and inexperienced girl – out in this big, exciting world! We drove there in a convoy of six vehicles. I was with Lolly, while his father drove the clients and Hope, Lolly's sister, was in another vehicle. The provisions were in a lorry driven by 'Uncle' Ernest. Unfortunately Ernest's car broke down so we drove on to the Fort Jameson hotel where we booked in and Lolly managed to get parts for the broken-down vehicle. Lolly and I then went back to rescue Uncle Ernest who was still sitting somewhere in the mountains.

Working on the car was difficult, with the unrelenting heat. After Lolly and Ernest had finally fixed the vehicle, they decided they had a huge thirst and needed refreshment. They had brought with them some of the alcoholic brew made from peaches and brandy called mampoer which had its desired effect. Driving back, Lolly kept wanting to fall asleep. We decided that, although I had never actually driven a car, it would be safer if I were behind the steering wheel.

"You must stay awake to tell me what to do," I told Lolly, petrified at the thought of being in control of a car.

By this time it was the middle of the night. I managed to get the car into third gear before Lolly fell asleep. After that, there was no waking him! I didn't know how to change gears but the road was straight so I just kept driving. The car began to violently shake as we drove up a steep hill, but we somehow made it. Eventually I saw the lights of Fort Jameson and I knew that I wouldn't be able to drive into a built-up area. Lolly was sound asleep and waking him was no easy task. Fortunately, he was able to drive us the last little bit and we arrived in Fort Jameson at around 2am.

The next morning when the Americans heard the story from Lolly they applauded and said, "Well done!" I was proud. I had driven a car for the first time in my life. I consider this to be one of my first bush experiences.

We went on to Luangwa which is a beautiful national park. Africa was a paradise back then – beautiful and unspoilt with wide open spaces, teeming with wildlife. It was like living in a dream and I was privileged to experience it. We pitched our tents on the bank of the river. The game in this park is absolutely unbelievable. We were surrounded by animal noises. We could hear the elephants trumpeting and what sounded like the roaring of lions.

Hope, Lolly's sister, and I shared a *rondawel* (a circular dwelling with a conical thatched roof common throughout southern Africa). The walls did not reach the roof, but rather had a permanently open space of quite some distance between roof and wall. Also, there wasn't a door. We were really scared. We couldn't sleep, thinking elephants might come into our camp and trample our sleeping quarters during the night. I was surprised that Hope was also afraid because I thought she was 'bush-smart' and had often been on safaris, but she was as frightened as I was! Several times throughout the night we ran into the tents where clients were sleeping, waking them up shouting, "The elephants are here!" or, "Here are the lions!" Unlike us, they didn't seem to be afraid and chased us away, begging us to leave them alone and allowing them to go back to sleep.

The Luangwa Valley was a wake-up call to the magic and the wildness of Africa. It was an unforgettable experience. On one of the hunting excursions one of the hunters wounded a lion and it managed to escape. It's a hunting law that one doesn't leave a wounded animal to fend for itself in the bush, it needs to be tracked down and put out of its misery. I was invited to go with the hunting party to find the wounded lion. We had to leave the vehicles because of the terrain and walked for many kilometers, so far that I developed blisters on my feet. I was very frightened and any movement sent me scurrying for cover, hiding in the nearest available bush. I had never seen wild animals before. Suddenly I noticed what I thought was a big branch lying on the ground. It moved and my fear was unbelievable. It wasn't a branch, it was a python! It had been burnt in a bush fire but it was still very much alive. To my horror, Lolly's father decided he would take the python with us. So off we went again, Lolly's father carrying the huge snake.

One of the eagle-eyed scouts spotted evidence of the wounded lion. The chase was on. Because of my blistered feet I could not join the final pursuit so I was left in the middle of the bush in a dry river bed with an African tracker for company. When my companion realised that they had not left us a gun, he hurriedly took off after the others and I was left there all alone, unable to follow. I started to cry. I cried as I had never cried before. I didn't know what to do. I didn't know what to expect or what dangers lay in wait for me. I was absolutely petrified. It was my first bush experience and I felt that Africa was cruel and that everybody was heartless. It was beginning to get dark and there was no one near. I was paralysed with fear.

Eventually the hunters found the wounded lion and shot it. The vehicle couldn't get to where the lion was so they had to carry it back. Then they remembered me and found me sitting in my river bed sobbing my eyes out. I still had to walk back

Ala's Story

to the car – blisters and all, only too relieved to be in safe company.

Lolly's father had walked to the nearest village and managed to buy a bag in which to put the snake. The lion went on the back of the truck, but the python had to go inside, with us. Lolly was driving and I was in the passenger seat. All I could think about on that trip was, "My God! I hope the python does not get out of the bag."

With the experience I now have I would not behave as I did then. Going on the trip I didn't realise what went on in the bush. I experienced all sorts of emotions – fear, tears, and wanting to see it all, trying to be brave and not managing too well. Lolly's sister, Hope, wasn't much help. She was as frightened as I was. When I saw that python coming towards me I thought it would be my death. This was my introduction to the African bush.

The python did actually get out of the bag – and while we were driving! But fortunately I didn't know about it at the time.

When we got back to the camp I was not worried about the lion, all I could say to the Americans was, "The pyfon! The pyfon!" My tongue was unable to get around the word correctly. The Americans didn't know what I was talking about so they all rushed to see what a 'pyfon' was. In the meantime the python had escaped from the bag. The head was between the clutch and the brake. Lolly knew what had happened but had not said anything because he knew how terrified I would be. When I heard that it had nearly escaped from the bag while we were driving I just went cold. They kept it in the caravan while we were in Luangwa Valley and took it out for fresh air every day. Because it had been burnt it couldn't move very quickly so when it did escape on one of its exercise routines, it was not too difficult to recapture even when it once managed to cross the river. The people in the camp teased me and called me the 'pyfon' because everywhere I went I wanted to know where the 'pyfon' was. The snake was not the only creature in our camp. There was also a lion cub. I was able to touch and, when I felt safe enough, to stroke it. They told me that the mother had been shot. It was an orphan and needed to be looked after. Even though I was often really frightened it was a wonderful experience – seeing the wild animals and the beautiful African bush.

Luangwa was paradise. It was like walking in a dream, with wonderful sunsets and colours never before imagined. As the sun went down on the horizon the sky turned a brilliant red tinted with oranges and yellows. The colours were reflected in the water, making it a river of rich golden hues. I found it was the beauty that really appealed to me. Seeing those sunsets in the late afternoons made me feel that Africa was a magic continent. The animals, too, were amazing. I must have seen just about every species of animal that it was possible to see in the African bush. In the Polish camp in Lusaka we had been secluded and only saw the occasional snake, but never antelope and other beautiful creatures. I even thought the lions to be majestic beasts although I was afraid of them.

After my ordeal in the bush I stayed in the camp and did not venture out on any more hunting adventures. Hope and I used to try to sleep in the day so that at night we could keep a patrol. Our paranoid fear of wild animals trespassing into our camp precluded our getting any sleep at night. We sat on our little camp beds in the incomplete rondawel with our feet up, looking out for anything that might venture in. This lasted for the duration of the two weeks we spent on safari. We were in the camp with the python and the lion cub with lions coming near and elephants trumpeting, all the night sounds that one hears in the bush. They were all so strange to me and even when the jackal called I would cringe. All the animals I had never previously known were suddenly very close. The snake was a problem but if I wanted to be associated with Lolly it was something I would have to get used to. There was fear of the unknown and reluctance to venture out, but also the charm and beauty of Africa which had become a huge drawcard for me although I wasn't sure whether I ever wanted to be back in the bush again.

After the adventures in the Luangwa Valley our safari went to Lake Nyasa in Nyasaland. By now I had fallen madly in love with Africa. I felt that I would never be able to leave. It was so totally different to any of the places I remembered from my childhood.

The safari was for some Americans who had paid Lolly's father to take them trophy hunting so perhaps this might be a good time to talk about my feelings on hunting. In those days, shooting rabbits and going on hunting trips did not denote the concepts of ecology as perceived nowadays. Hunters were appreciated by the world, and there wasn't conservation as there is today. If a boy shot a leopard at a young age he was considered a hero. That's why going on hunting safaris was something special. I didn't (and still don't) like the killing aspect, but there was an image of bravery and excitement that was associated with the hunters. Today there is an emphasis on conservation. I always try to think about what is wrong and what is acceptable, but inevitably I go back to the beginning of the world when God said, "I created the creatures and I put them there for you to look after and live off."

There is always a reason and a plan for everything. Nowadays some people seem to go overboard with conservation and forget that there are times when it is necessary, as a last resort, to cull herds or hunt for whatever reason. The reality in Africa is that animals compete for space and survival. Wildlife will ultimately be the loser unless humans can learn to co-exist with it. Failure to do so could result in the disappearance of African wildlife – a decidedly unacceptable option.

The engagement

Back in Livingstone, Mother and I were very happy living in a little cottage. Lolly, who was living on his own, could not be bothered to cook his own food so he asked Mother if he could come and have meals with us. We agreed, but when he informed us that he only ate chicken and fish, I put my foot down and told him he would have to eat what we ate, or go hungry. Meat was cheaper at that time. You could buy fillet steak for one shilling and six pence a pound. Chicken and fish were more expensive. We didn't have much money and were trying to build up our lives, so were not prepared to pander to Lolly's expensive whims.

In those days Livingstone offered a colonial-type experience. The economy was going through a post-war boom and there were plenty of opportunities for people to start a business and make financial headway. Anyone wanting to get anything started had it relatively easy, provided they identified a gap and were prepared to work hard to achieve their goals. We were living at the right time in the right place when, given the chance and the will, you could get almost anything done. We worked hard and started to see progress in our business.

I finally agreed to become engaged to Lolly after he produced a ring one evening. Our engagement didn't disrupt our working routine and we continued with the business. We increased our number of cars and the tourism business took off. There were no launches operating out of Livingstone on the Zambezi River; there was only one on the Southern Rhodesian side that was run by the railways from the Victoria Falls Hotel. We saw the opportunity and started to bring in travel agents and build up the launch business from Livingstone on the northern side of the falls.

We had lots of friends and a great social life. We went for trips on the Zambezi and had lots of picnics. Life was for living and I still feel privileged when I think back on those days.

We were not aware of poverty (although I'm sure it was there). Servants were commonplace and life was easy. Everybody was friendly and picnics were the place to be seen.

Even though I was engaged (or perhaps because of it), I felt the need for a little freedom. I also wanted to see more of Africa. I had a Polish school friend, Zosia, who lived in Abercorn (in the north of Northern Rhodesia not far from Lake Tanganyika). I travelled up there and spent a week with her. At that time her husband, Roy, was working with the police service. She was, and is, a good friend and we still communicate. After my stay in Abercorn I went for a five-day cruise on a steam boat on Lake Tanganyika – from one side to the other. There

Me at the
Victoria Falls

were many young people on the trip and it proved to be a riot of fun. We went out on small boats, went diving and there was a party every single night. I made friends easily – what with my beautiful long hair and unusual accent, I went far. After disembarking from the steam boat, I went to Kigoma and to Dar Es Salaam by train. I stayed in a hotel at Dar Es Salaam and I hired a little boat to explore the ships and the harbour. For the first time in years, I was beginning to feel independent.

From Dar Es Salaam I flew to Zanzibar. On the plane I met a guy from the BBC and made friends with two British teachers. The BBC man said he was doing a broadcast in Zanzibar and the company that had commissioned him was providing a car at the airport. He invited us to join him for the ride into town, as well as have lunch with an Arab family he was meeting and to join him on a tour of the

Ala's Story

island. The teachers and I joined him and it was a lovely experience. But, after a few days, I began to run a bit short of money. I sent Lolly a message from Dar es Salaam asking him to forward me some money from my salary as I wanted to fly back home in the newest plane. I had booked a boat trip from Dar es Salaam to Durban, which proved to be wonderful as I met lots of interesting people. When we arrived in Durban Lolly was waiting for me. He'd had enough. Instead of sending me the money he'd driven to Durban to meet me at the boat! He said, "Enough is enough! Now you're coming home with me." So that was that.

The trip on my own endorsed the realisation that as a teenager I had lost so much of my life. But now the world was opening up and I had discovered the dual pleasure of freedom and friends; it felt as if I was just beginning to start life. I wanted to enjoy myself with friends and fulfill myself at work. I even enjoyed meeting the police force when the guys used to come into the office for coffee and I found the bush people quite fascinating. I was having fun and perhaps I did not want this stage of my life to end. This may well explain why our engagement lasted for such a long time. I had postponed marriage by stipulating that we had to have a house first, but I really don't think I was ready to settle down. The prerequisite of having a house was perhaps a subconscious ruse to enjoy my freedom for just a little bit longer. Lolly and I had our ups and downs and there were times when I met other men – like a very charming Frenchman – when I seriously thought that I should not be engaged and thinking of marriage. I still carried some of the insecurities I had experienced when I was struggling to survive. Lolly used to admire me because I had such beautiful long, blonde plaits. I think this was a problem – was it me, the 'real' me – or was it simply my lovely, long blonde hair that attracted him?

My brother, Janusz, also lived in Livingstone with us and it was here that he discovered major temptations. He found it very strange that shops would let new consignments of goods remain unattended on the sidewalk for days. In those days the crime rate was very low. Janusz, however, saw this as a heaven-sent opportunity to acquire things that he found desirable. He particularly coveted a radiogram left standing outside a certain shop, so one night he decided to make it his own, which he did and seemed to get away with it. He also helped himself to a gun which he 'borrowed'. The owner missed it and he reported it to the police. When the police showed a growing interest in Janusz and the missing gun, he hid it in the servants' quarters. This time his luck had run out. The gun was traced to him and he was arrested. At that time my mother was away on holiday. She needed to rest and I didn't want to distress her so I didn't tell her about Janusz's latest troubles. I bailed him out and, although I was only 18 years old, I went to court to speak in his defence. I said he was guilty in every way but I wanted the judge to consider his past. I pointed out that he was the son of a judge and had been brought up in a wonderful family with the best of everything. When we ended up in Russia he learned that the only way to survive was to steal. It was what he had to do. He learned to be a survivor from a very early age. I simply told the judge the truth. I said that Janusz admitted to stealing, but he did it without the realisation that it was wrong. The judge let him off with a severe warning and a caning.

Janusz remembers a young girl, Stefa, who lived with us because she couldn't find other accommodation. He had stolen the gun from her boyfriend. Of course, I also remember Stefa because she's the one who taught Lolly all the Polish swear-words!

Janusz always seemed to have a great affinity for animals. He bought a leopard from an African chap living near the Zambezi. The leopard must have been about two months old. Janusz brought it home. He used to take it for drives when he borrowed one of Lolly's cars. The leopard behaved like a dog. He would put his paws out the car window and loved to feel the wind blowing his ears back. They used to drive down to Victoria Falls where there were lots of guinea fowl that the leopard enjoyed chasing, not that he ever caught one. The beautiful animal also held a huge fascination for girls – what a plus for Janusz!

Lolly, too, had a leopard as a pet. By that time he was living in the Post Office house where he shared a room with another man. This house had a large verandah enclosed with mosquito netting where the leopard could live in safety. One day the leopard escaped from its verandah enclosure. Lolly wasn't at home at the time. Two dear old ladies were sitting having tea in the garden. The leopard thought it might be a good idea to visit the ladies. His sudden appearance caused quite a commotion! Tables were overturned, cups and saucers went flying and there were screams and shouts because the ladies thought they were about to be savaged by a wild animal. They quickly sought shelter in the house. After this Lolly was forced to move the leopard to our cottage. It wasn't allowed to scare any more old ladies! We had to keep him tied up in the garden because there was a busy street just outside and we had no other place to keep him. The police heard the story of the leopard frightening the two old women and they traced it to our house and came to arrest it. The leopard was hiding in a tree with branches that overhung the garden path. Thinking this was glorious fun, he promptly jumped onto one of the policemen when he walked under the tree. We were told that we couldn't keep it in our garden so we took it to a farm where it could stay in peace without being harassed by policemen or tempted by old ladies. Unfortunately it killed a calf and the farmer had to shoot it, which was very sad.

About this time Janusz also had a pet baboon. He remembers it fondly, "Every time a female came anywhere near him he used to play with himself. The odd thing was he did it with his feet. A fascinating accomplishment. One which humans would find near impossible."

Ala's Story

Another memorable event for us while we were living in Livingstone was when we were involved in the making of the film, *Duel in the Jungle*. We were contracted to supply all their needs, including the mokoros (boats hollowed out of tree trunks, made by the local people). We also had to provide the men who knew how to stand up and row the mokoros. We retained African singers, supplied food, found accommodation, organised the transport – virtually everything. It was a huge undertaking and very good business. There were some big name stars working on the movie like Jeanne Crane and Dana Andrews who both came from America and David Farrar from England. Dana was the biggest *dronkie* (alcoholic) you could imagine. He had been thrown out of every hotel and police club in Livingstone, literally the entire extent of places to buy drinks back then. His drinking was a huge problem. We even snapped a pic of him sleeping it off at the bottom of a mokoro.

Dana Andrews asleep in the mokoro

I remember that Jeanne Crane was really charming. Her husband, however, was awful – full of himself and forever blowing his own trumpet. Jeanne was beautiful but he wasn't a nice person. I used to wonder how such a lovely lady ended up with such a lout.

We certainly enjoyed some good moments while we were working on the film. One scene I remember was when Jeanne Crane was walking through the rainforest near the Victoria Falls. Lolly had climbed up a tree which overhung her path, positioned in one of the branches. The idea was that as she passed under the tree Lolly was going to lower a snake to give her a huge fright. I don't think she was doing much acting when actually confronted by the snake – she screamed her lungs out – although it was firmly held by Lolly. This snake lived in a crate which we kept at our little cottage. I remember keeping lots of heavy stones on top of the crate to stop the snake getting out. I still have a healthy respect for snakes.

It was a great film about an insurance man coming to Africa to investigate a dubious claim. Ironically, the 'good guy' hero who eventually won the fair maiden (Jeanne Crane) was Dana Andrews and the nice David Farrar was the villain. All sorts of things happened in the movie and Janusz and Clyde had to double for the stars in the dangerous parts. Once Lolly, Clyde and an African man, acting as doubles, were coming down the very dangerous Katambora rapids in a boat. They were supposed to move down the river in front of the camera, dropping Clyde off at one point and the African guy at another. We waited and waited for the boat to appear but it never came. We were getting quite anxious when someone came running towards us, shouting that he had seen the boat capsize. There was a big panic. But this is exactly what had happened: the boat had turned turtle. Lolly swam to the island and Clyde helped the African man swim to safety. Everyone was safe, although that section of filming had to be redone.

Another time, when they were shooting a scene on the rapids, the co-director was on the boat and, although he had repeatedly been told to sit down, he arrogantly insisted on standing. Clyde, Lolly's brother, who was playing double for Dana Andrews in this particular scene, was also in the boat as well as an African fella. The boat got into difficulties and they had to try to turn it around. Once again it capsized and they all landed in the water. Tony Kelly, the co-director, shouted above the roar of the water, "Don't worry about me, I can swim!" Clyde then concentrated his efforts on saving the African actor who was unable to swim and in danger of drowning. Clyde managed to drag him to safety. We were all standing on the bank watching. Tony waved to us and then dramatically disappeared under the water. He was gone. Later they found his wallet and his socks. He had simply vanished in front of everyone's eyes – his body was never found. There was no doubt that he had been taken by a crocodile. There is an unbelievable feeling of horror in witnessing something like this. One minute you see someone and everything seems to be safe and then, suddenly,

Ala's Story

there's nothing.

The filming was full of other exciting events. Once Janusz, doubling for Jeanne Crane, had to swim in the rapids. In order to resemble her, he had to wear an identical dress to one she wore. I have a photograph of the two of them – Jeanne Crane with her gorgeous legs and Janusz all bandy. Obviously he had to have bosoms so we used two oranges. Jeanne was quite insulted by this and said, "Those do not do justice to my shape!" So paw paws were used instead. Because Janusz and other actors had to swim in the rapids for the scene, they threw sticks of dynamite in first in order to scare the crocodiles away. Janusz had to hold hands with Dana and David. I'm sure it is questionable whether or not he found that to be a stimulating experience!

I had to supply food for the actors and the crew every day. It was easy while we were filming around the falls. Sometimes there were as many as 60 people. Although I had no training, I didn't find it too difficult, even without deep freezers or adequate facilities.

One day when they had to do some film shoots at Katambora I had to cater for

Janusz doubling as Jeannie Crane

a huge crowd. They were going to be in the bush and there were absolutely no facilities. I decided the solution was to pre-pack all the lunches. Julie, a friend of mine, was a great help. By the time we had finished preparing and packing the food and were ready to leave there was only one vehicle left, an open jeep. We had to travel around 35 miles on a dry, dusty road. We carefully packed all the lunches into the jeep and off we went. We arrived at Katambora in good time and started to unpack. But what did we find? Everything was covered with sand from the dusty trip. There was nothing to do except wash all the food in the river – every piece of meat and chicken, each leaf of salad. Ignorance was indeed bliss as everyone seemed to enjoy the lunches without ever suspecting that their food had been in the river which they considered to be polluted with bilharzia.

Another river incident was when we ran out of fresh water. We (the locals) always drank river water from the Zambezi rapids as we felt sure that no bilharzia could survive such fast-flowing water but for visitors we had special filtered water kept in flasks. But this time I was desperate so I went around to a point of the island where I thought no-one could see me, and filled all the flasks from the rapids. Unfortunately I was seen and my actions were reported to the director, a Lithuanian Jew. This man could hardly speak English. He was really cross and said, "You want to kill all my children? They will all get hysterics." No one got sick or died laughing. They all survived.

Escapades

Janusz worked with us in Livingstone. We often had rich American tourists from luxury boat cruises who used to fly in to view Victoria Falls. Janusz always looked for wealthy older women. He'd make a huge fuss over them and then tell them how poorly he was doing, working for his sister who abused him and wouldn't pay him a salary. The old dears would usually feel so sorry for him, giving him big tips and offering him things like world cruises, luxury and coddling, while promising to look after him and take him away from his unkind sister. His response? He'd come home and say, "Gosh! She looked terrible! I couldn't spend another day with that one!" What a rogue!

Janusz also had the privilege of meeting all the young girls who went on our cruises. Once there was a young Rhodesian girl who was studying physical training in New York. Her parents had a clothing factory in Bulawayo. He met her while she was on holiday at Victoria Falls. In no time Janusz had swept her off her feet. He drove her everywhere and took her to cocktail parties. He entertained her and took her to Wankie, a town around 67 miles away, just for dinner. Her holiday ended and she went back to Bulawayo. She was a Jewish girl and Alec Slatzkin, our mayor, who was also Jewish, came to me and said, "Ala, do you know a Russian prince living in Livingstone?" to which I replied, "No, I had never met a Russian prince." He then said, "Friends of mine from Bulawayo phoned to tell me that their daughter was here on holiday and that she was entertained by a Russian prince, so they asked me to find out who he is and what he does."

About a week or two later the mayor again phoned and said, "You know who the Russian prince is? It's your brother." I asked how he had found out. He said, "I was in Bulawayo with my friends. They took me out to dinner and who did I happen to see on the dance floor? Erica with the Russian 'prince' and guess who he was? It was Janusz."

You cannot imagine what that brother of mine got away with. I used to despair at his antics. I really disapproved of his lifestyle. I used to tear my hair out. Once he had a girlfriend named Thora. That relationship lasted on and off for quite a while – as usual. First Thora, then someone else, then Thora again. One day Thora came to see me and said Janusz was going out with the boys that night and asked what was I doing. I had to be at the motel that evening. We now owned the motel and I used to relieve the manager so he could have the occasional night off. Thora asked if she could come with me. Naturally I agreed. What I didn't know was that 'the boys' with whom Janusz was supposed to be having a night out was a beauty pageant winner, 'Miss Kroonstad' from South Africa, whose prize for winning the title was a trip to Victoria Falls. Needless to say, Janusz had 'found' her. She was booked into the motel. As we drove up to the motel Thora suddenly jumped out of the car before I brought it to a stand-still. I didn't know what was happening. Thora had seen Janusz pull into the carpark with Miss Kroonstad at his side. Thora was like a demon. She attacked the glamourous girl and tried to claw her face. The two had a glorious fist fight. Janusz desperately tried to separate them and I helplessly stood around, not knowing what to do. I was furious, especially with Janusz. Anyway, he eventually managed to tear them off each other and drove off with Miss Kroonstad in the car. Thora was hysterical, so much so that she had to stay at the motel that night. When I got home I confronted Janusz and had my say.

"Plenty," mumbles Janusz, who had been listening to me telling this story, "But I don't remember Ala actually beating me with a stick that day!"

Although in no way regretting his past, Janusz tried to explain away his actions by saying, "My time in Livingstone was the best of my life. We had a fantastic life. I would go to Wankie Game Reserve for two or three days at a time with tour groups. I don't know what it was – my exotic accent or looks – but women literally swarmed around me – married, single, whatever. I suppose if I was a woman I would have been called a 'slut'. But being a man I got away with it. It was the best time of my life. Of course I loved Livingstone for other reasons, such as the beauty of the place and our grand lifestyle. But I guess the women made it particularly memorable." Janusz must have been pretty good at whatever he did because most of the women came back for more!

For me, as well as for my brother, Africa held so much charm. It was unspoiled and raw. We had nothing when we first arrived here. With hard work, vision and determination we were able to achieve so much. Today people don't have the same opportunities. Unfortunately, my brother had good looks and he made a lot of money. This made it so easy for him to get women. Before I married I wouldn't dare have affairs. There was always the fear of falling pregnant. If one fell pregnant before marriage it was considered a disgrace. The only incident that I remember concerning men other than Lolly was with a Polish pen pal. He was in the army and we never actually met. He planned to emigrate to Australia and wanted Mother and me to join him there. Mother was quite keen, mostly because he was Polish, but the idea of moving to Australia didn't appeal to me – partly because it would have meant starting life all over again. Secondly, I felt I didn't really know the man.

But Janusz was spoiled and women chased him. At that time it was difficult for me to understand why they ran after him. In those days men were supposed to do the chasing. His response to my scepticism was: "You always ask me what women see in me and, if you were not my sister, I'd tell you." The possible disgrace of sex before marriage was not something that worried Janusz. He indulged in many affairs. How his lady friends managed not to fall pregnant I don't know, because there was no such thing as a contraceptive pill in those days. Also, there weren't concerns about AIDS then either. He was a very naughty boy which he now admits. He was mad about life. He probably thought he should live for each day because he didn't know what would happen the next. I am convinced that his lifestyle and loose morals were a product of his childhood. He learned to be suspicious about tomorrow, so took what he could when it was available. I compensated for the nightmares of our life in Siberia by raiding the fridge, while he blocked out his insecurities by sleeping with women. We didn't have psychiatrists to help us deal with our trauma so we had to cope as best we could on our own.

Crocodile hunting
and other adventures

Women were surprisingly not the only thing Janusz found stimulating. Crocodile hunting was equally exciting and proved to be an extremely lucrative business. Janusz often went hunting with John Coleman, a game warden at the Victoria Falls. Between them I think they must have shot almost all the crocodiles in the Zambezi River! Lolly had a licence to export the skins to France and other European countries and it wasn't necessary for him to check up on the permits of the people from whom he bought; still, poaching was illegal. Anyway, most people felt it was fine to shoot crocodiles because there were far too many of them and they made water sports on the river dangerous. The mass killing of the crocodiles did, however, upset the ecological balance of the river and suddenly there were far too many barbels swimming around because the predators were fewer. There are always consequences when humans interfere with nature.

Selling of skins was quite a good money spinner. Lolly paid fifteen shillings for an inch of skin, so if a crocodile was an average 35 inches one could make quite a bit. The sale of these skins funded Janusz's lifestyle especially as he used to stretch them as much as possible before selling to Lolly. He was able to indulge in convertibles, speedboats and lots and lots of champagne which was another particular weakness. When he was a bit short of skins he would sell what he had to Lolly and then 'pinch' them back and sell them again.

Once Janusz, Lolly and a Mr Barbosa went off to hunt crocodiles in Angola. Mr Barbosa went along as an interpreter. In Angola District Commissioners are known as the 'chef de poss' and – since they're in charge of an area – they can decide who should (or shouldn't) get a permit for hunting crocodiles. Lolly met this man and Mr Barbosa, a builder by trade, introduced himself as 'Engineer Barbosa'. Janusz looked him up and down in disbelief and enquired, "Since when were you an engineer? If you're an engineer I must be Dr Kuchcinski."

Lolly, always honest, simply introduced himself as 'Lolly Sussens'. The two hunters and 'engineer' Barbosa held a party and Janusz, as usual, impressed everybody. All this facilitated the permit and off they went up the river.

One day, while hunting up the river, they spied a boat approaching and its occupants bore a message from the commissioner. It said that his wife was seriously ill and in need of the attentions of a doctor. Would Dr Kuchcinski please come quickly? Lolly said, "Well you had better go and carry on your role as doctor because, if you don't, he will take the licence away. It will probably be malaria or else she's pregnant or has the 'flu. You'd better go and do something."

Ala's Story

So Janusz took the first aid box and went up to see the lady. Like always, he managed to charm her and gave her some aspirin. The next message from the commissioner was to invite the doctor and his party to join them for dinner because his wife was so much better. Perhaps Janusz had charmed away her malady.

Janusz tells a little more about this trip to Angola. "The river in Angola runs through a swamp which is about 20km wide. It's a long river and it winds a lot. At every bend there's a sand bank and on every sand bank there was a crocodile. Normally when hunting crocodiles it takes a whole night to get 10 to 15 crocodiles but by 8 or 9am we had to go back because we had already caught enough. We got lost once. There are moving islands and you can't find your way out of the place. After a late night and being on the river for hours we used to get quite sleepy. On this particular night Lolly was on the front seat and I was at the back – both of us fast asleep. The African chap who was with us was in the middle so that he was in the right position to spear any crocodiles we shot. It was always necessary to spear them once they had been shot or they would sink to the bottom of the muddy river and we wouldn't be able to find them. Anyway, this night Lolly and I were asleep. The African gent had a cap on because he was cold, but had also fallen asleep. When I woke up it was just getting light and there was a big crocodile with its mouth wide open going for the African guy's head which had lolled onto the side of the boat. Lolly also woke and pulled the man to safety just as the crocodile snapped his jaw shut. It sounded like a .303 going off. If Lolly hadn't pulled the man to safety he would have been headless!"

Janusz continues, "On the same day our African 'retriever' was nearly decapitated, we were running next to a bank and I saw a fish hanging in the tree. I pulled over to see what it was. I climbed out of the boat to investigate. As I got closer I fell into a crocodile trap. The local hunters dig a hole and put stakes in the bottom and cover the hole with sticks. They then hang a fish as bait. Fortunately the stakes missed my body but one did pierce my arm. Lolly pulled me out and I ended up with blood poisoning."

Barbosa was not very popular with Lolly and Janusz. He once fell off the boat and went underneath it. They did all they could to help him out, but he later claimed that they were trying to drown him because every time he attempted to come up they seemed to push him back in – of course he was bumping his head on the underside of the boat.

Back in Livingstone we had increased the number of vehicles we owned and had bought another launch and a couple more boats. Lolly moved his jetty to the Maramba River which was also on the Northern Rhodesian side of the Falls. He also brought in a very large crocodile for people to see when they came in on the boat. Janusz recounts the story of the crocodile: "We caught a 15-foot long crocodile which we installed near the launch so that people could see it and photograph it before they left for their trips. The creature also came in useful when Lolly's brother decided to shoot a film about crocodiles. One particular shot was of an African 'actor' going to the water and being taken by a crocodile. Clyde was supposed to jump into the water with a knife at the crucial moment and slay the crocodile because shooting it would be dangerous in case the man was shot by mistake. They wired the mouth of the crocodile and returned it to the water. The actor approached the river to fill his bucket. He had a rope tied to his feet so that we could pull him into the water with a jerk which would look as if the crocodile had taken him. It would have been very effective. But the crocodile did not want to play. It refused to move. It lay very still on the bank. I yelled, 'Poke the thing in the back', Clyde obliged and the crocodile went mad. It twisted and turned and beat the ground with its tail. The onlookers were convinced that it would break the wire and kill someone. Fortunately all this was caught on film and it proved to be a great success and no one got hurt."

Crocodile hunting was not the only pastime that Janusz enjoyed. Lolly also introduced him to elephant hunting. On their first trip they drove out in their little green jeep, met up with Clyde and went off in search of elephants. They walked for days looking for the giant beasts and eventually found three which they shot. After a further three days of hunting, the men returned to the site of the dead elephants. They found the creatures still lying in the sun. There were a lot of villages around that area and, of course, the locals came for the meat. The smell was awful and the elephants had swollen and blown up in the 40 degree temperature. Clyde climbed on top of one of them with his gun. The local people were all standing around with their pangas ready to hack out the meat and one of them must have accidentally chopped into the stomach of the elephant. There was a terrific explosion and Clyde fell off. It was like dynamite. One of the local men fell and broke his arm. But the rest started reaping the meat. In the space of one and a half hours there was nothing left.

I did experience many anxious hours over the escapades of Lolly and Janusz. Once Lolly was asked to deliver a 50-foot boat from above the Devil's Cataract at Victoria Falls to Katambora. To transport the boat by road would have been very expensive and time consuming. The alternative was that they took the boat up the river. At the time the river was in flood so there was plenty of water, but it would mean sailing against the current up the very fast-moving Katambora rapids. It was a journey that no one had previously tried and incredibly dangerous. Lolly remembers seeing a partly submerged tree and glancing at his watch, "Half an hour later we were still trying to pass that tree. It took forever to move a few meters!" They ultimately succeeded in their journey, but I spent the time expecting to see two lifeless bodies and a lot of bits of boat rushing over the Victoria Falls.

Of course women played an important role in Janusz's life. He likes to tell the story of one of the woman he became involved with. I remember this particular lady quite well especially because I had to get the police to stop him running away with her. He was about 17 at the time.

"I became a saw doctor sharpening saws for the mills," recalls Janusz. "This was also about the time that I started poaching crocodiles because Lolly was paying so much for the skins. It was a pretty busy period because it also involved a woman. She was about seven years my senior. She simply loved to go to bed. Anyway, the repeated exertions resulted in that eventually I was only skin and bone. I looked like a skeleton. The affair lasted for about a year. That was until Ala managed to put a stop to it."

I was so shocked by Janusz's way of life. I would never have thought of doing anything like he did.

Shortly after I succeeded in breaking up his affair with the older divorcée, Janusz met Pam. By then he was 19 years old. They often went out on his motorbike. She, too, was older than him, and he managed to get her pregnant. In those times the correct thing to do was to get married. It was a very small wedding – our mother, Pam's mother, Lolly and myself.

Pam was short, about five feet tall, but very beautiful. They had a little girl, Teresa, and moved to Lusaka where Janusz managed to find a job. He was still quite skinny from his previous amorous exertions but all went well with them for a short while.

Janusz and Pam lived together in Lusaka for about three years after which Pam returned to Livingstone because the marriage wasn't working out.

It was while Janusz was in Lusaka that Lolly and I got married.

Mother, Pam, Janusz and Pam's mother at the wedding

The Wedding

Lolly and I were engaged for seven years – off and on! I wasn't serious about getting married. I loved Lolly very much. But I also loved people; I loved mixing with people and I loved meeting people and we had a wonderful circle of friends. I had previously told Lolly that I didn't think that we should get married until we had a house. But the money was going into the business so there was nothing left to build a home.

Life was just great. But we did take our responsibilities seriously. I can remember one New Year's Eve when all our friends went to a party and we had to work. I took phone calls all night while Lolly drove the taxi. We worked well together. The business was growing and we were progressing so finally, no getting out of it any more, we built a house. My mother was not very keen on my marrying a South African. She would have preferred me to have married a Pole. She endured a lot of stress over this. Needless to say she later grew to love Lolly very much.

Before finally taking the walk down the aisle, we decided to go on a safari with two of our friends, John and Claire. Lolly was too busy to start the journey with us, so the three of us set off for Tanganyika. Lolly was to join us in Kenya. Just before we got to Kenya I decided that I would cut off my hair. When Lolly met up with us he was so upset about my hair and accused me of cutting off his 'love'! In Nairobi there was a lot of fear about the Mau Mau, an anti-colonial group responsible for some horrific murders in the area. All the hotel staff where we were staying had been arrested on suspicion of being part of the Mau Mau uprising, then at its peak. The Tree Tops hotel was burned down the day before we arrived. Claire and I immediately started helping the hotel with its catering. I remember attending a dance there and being very aware of the guns in the holsters of the officers with whom I danced.

On our way to the Belgian Congo we had to drive on a narrow road through a high pass. We didn't know this road only carried one-way traffic. One day the traffic travelled north and the next it went south. As luck would have it we arrived on the wrong day. We were told, however, that we would be able to carry on with our journey after 6pm. We found a good place to stop and Lolly decided that he would use the time to service our vehicle. I took a blanket and a book and settled myself comfortably under a tree. Engrossed in the book, I was surprised when Lolly shouted at me to remain perfectly still. I looked up and saw a huge black mamba right above me. I always had a fear of snakes and was petrified! Anyway, the dreadful thing eventually slithered off and I was able to run to the safety of the car. Our safari also took us to Uganda and then home to prepare for the wedding.

Ala's Story

About two weeks before the wedding Lolly's father arrived in Livingstone and said, "You are not allowed to marry a Catholic girl. You have to make another plan. It can't be a Catholic wedding."

This was funny because Lolly's brother, Ian, had also married a Catholic – a French girl, Odette. Lolly came to me and said, "We have to change the wedding plans."

I was a very strong-minded person and said, "In that case the wedding is off." That certainly made him think!

Despite all our parents' objections we sent out wedding invitations to about 350 people – it was a huge wedding because friendships were paramount and everyone knew one another in Livingstone in those days.

After seven years there was a lot of speculation among our friends as to whether or not this marriage would ever take place. They were pleasantly surprised when we announced that the house was complete and we could now get married. The invitations had already gone out when Lolly developed appendicitis. It was an emergency. The doctor who operated on him, Dr Major, always used to fortify himself with a good tot of something strong before he operated. Those were the days! So after his tot of whisky he operated and left some wadding behind in the wound. A few days after the operation while we were on a walk, I suddenly saw something red streaming down Lolly's leg. It was blood. He had an infection and that took a long time to heal. He was very, very sick.

Although Lolly was still not well we continued with the wedding preparations. In those days there was no such thing as having caterers like we have today, so all my friends came in every day to our empty house (we had no furniture). They stayed for the entire week and we baked and cooked for 350 people! It was great. There were fire engines, huge vehicles, cars and lorries parked outside on the driveway. Lolly lay on our one single bed in the bedroom while all the activities were going on in the kitchen. I sometimes wonder if one can still have friends like that these days. Friends also made my dress and those for the bridesmaids. I had four bridesmaids and a flower girl. They all wore white and carried red roses to reflect the national colours of Poland. I had a white dress and carried white lilies. In spite of their objections to a Catholic wedding, Lolly's father and brother both came to the wedding in the Catholic church. It was very hot on our wedding day. I remember standing in the church with perspiration running down my legs. I was quite a plump bride which didn't help the heat situation. Poor Lolly was still *eina* (sore) and the worst was when the doctor said to him, "I did this on purpose actually, so that I could take your place."

Lolly wobbled down to the altar but didn't really enjoy the wedding party. I had the fun. I spent the afternoon in the pub singing with the boys, it was fantastic! It was a real Rhodesian full-of-fun wedding. The food was terrific, the company great. In fact, everything was great.

After the wedding Lolly and I and a bunch of friends travelled to Bulawayo in convoy. From Bulawayo, Lolly and I travelled to the Cape, in South Africa, for our honeymoon. I can't remember much about my honeymoon but I do remember that Lolly was not very well so it was probably not quite as memorable as it should have been.

Back home in Livingstone our house was always open to anyone who needed a meal or a place to stay. This was the suburban Rhodesian way of life. We always had people around. Friends came from farms and even from as far away as Botswana. The place buzzed. I never knew how many to expect for lunch. Fortunately Paul, my cook, was able to cope with the situation. He would ask how many people were expected and I would usually say four. Later I would have to change the number of guests to ten, but Paul took it in his stride and would say that it was okay because he always cooked enough for 15. That was the way I

Our wedding,
2 October 1954

Ala's Story

liked it. We were very hospitable. We had many friends, some are still our friends. I always say that you can buy material things but you can't buy friends, they are blessings who are sent to you. Sometimes, instead of eating at home, we would all meet at the launch jetty where Lolly might have had two or three trips, then we would have a *braai* (barbeque) together.

Janusz's wife, Pam, and two-year-old daughter, Teresa, arrived from Lusaka, claiming that Janusz did not have accommodation for them because he was living in a caravan. At that time John Slade was working for us. He was a really good worker and we were pleased to have him. One day he came to us and said, "I'm sorry but I have to give you notice. I have to leave."

I asked him why and added, "We do wish you well and would be sorry to see you go, but why do you need to leave?" To which John blurted out, "Well, I have fallen in love with Pam."

I asked if Janusz knew about this. He said, "No, but he's coming this weekend so we'll have to tell him."

I felt terrible that my brother was going to receive this appalling news. When Janusz came John said, "Janusz, I am very sorry, but I have to tell you that Pam and I are in love and we want to go away together."

Impulsively Janusz hugged him and said, "You're my best friend – and you've done me the biggest favour of my life."

Janusz thought it the best thing that had ever happened. He had grown tired of

Our house in Livingstone

his wife and was only too ready to regain his freedom (and, by the way, John is still a great friend).

According to Janusz there was only one woman that he truly loved as a wife or mistress. She was a French lady – very beautiful with a lovely figure. She was tragically killed in a car accident and he was extremely sad. This happened while he was on his own in Lusaka. It affected his whole life. So he returned to Livingstone for good and I offered him a job as a mechanic, knowing he had completed his apprenticeship in Lusaka. He maintained our fleet of cars. He took the launches up to the islands, driving clients and conducting tours to Livingstone and taking control of cruises on the river.

In the early days, before John eventually went off with Pam, he and Janusz shared a room. Interestingly, there wasn't any animosity between the two guys over Pam. John and Pam later went up north and Janusz lost touch with his little daughter. Much later, Pam's divorce from Janusz went through and she married her second husband. The sad part was that I wanted to adopt Teresa. Pam refused and got Janusz to sign papers under false pretenses saying that she was sending the child to her grandmother for a holiday. In fact she sent her to England to a granny where she lived for 15 years. She was separated from both her parents and was very unhappy. What a pity I was not allowed to have her. She would have had a happy home and attended a good school in Livingstone.

The business was doing well. I can't remember the year, but we took over all the Victoria Falls launches. We set up our offices at the Falls. I think that the reason we made such a success of our business is because I have a God-given gift. I'm not artistic, I can't sew on buttons but I can be creative in business. I love being with people and my profession, business and professional commitments always come first.

We didn't want to have children immediately, although I was 24 when I married and Lolly was 32. I knew what I wanted in life so we didn't have children right away. Our life together was good and I didn't feel children would add to our happiness at that time.

We approached everything with a positive attitude. We had to buy vehicles on hire purchase but felt safe doing this as the tourism industry was growing. God was really good to us. We were blessed with lots of wonderful things like good travel agents who sent us lots of clients and other influential people who believed in us. The hospitality business started then and it has been part of my life ever since. Through my work I've met all sorts of people – from the dirtiest tramps to royalty. I love a challenge and this way of life presented a continuous challenge. It's important to always be sure of your success – with this belief you can go through life and get to the top without hurting people. Truly successful living is driven by the belief that you can make it.

Family matters

About two years after our wedding we started learning to fly. Every day something new – just like the young people of today. We became friendly with Dr Nolly Zaloumis, who later became very influential in the South African wildlife industry, helping establish the St Lucia Reserve. He had studied in Johannesburg and started a dental practice in the same building as our office. He was a real live wire. He wasn't married so we invited him to join us for meals in the evening. After they had finished eating, Lolly and Nolly would sit in armchairs on either side of me and go to sleep. I would happily talk to myself until I realised that they weren't listening. The three of us decided we wanted to learn to fly. In the evenings we used to go to the airport for lessons from our flying instructors. Altogether, there were five of us attending the lectures – the three of us and another married couple. I was very embarrassed when I registered that only three of us were listening to the lecture. As usual, the men on either side of me had fallen asleep. I kicked them under the table. We had a very good flying instructor. I only had one scare: we were flying one day and the cockpit filled up with smoke and my instructor had to make an emergency landing. I enjoyed flying and wanted to continue but discovered I was pregnant. Lolly insisted that we start a family. I wasn't very keen. So that was the end of my flying story. None of us completed the course because my two guys never cooperated very well.

When we employed Janusz on his return from Lusaka we also hired a man called Stewart Campbell. The two of them admired and respected me but never listened to me and did their own thing. They went for the good times, but were delightful company.

Stewart Campbell. He was a character! He wore his hair long which was not really the fashion of the day, and was quite eccentric. We once went to a party at the Falls Tearoom on the banks of the Zambezi River and we were all dancing. Near us was a guy with long, scraggly hair. He worked for the opposition boat trips on the Southern Rhodesian side. Stewart asked me if he looked as terrible as this guy with the hair. I said, "Stewart, you look much worse."

The next morning we saw Stewart getting out of his car. It was very hot and he had a huge hat on as well as a big scarf around his neck. I could not help thinking, 'My goodness, what could be wrong with him?' So I asked, "Stewart are you not well?" to which he replied, "No, I'm okay." So I said, "Why are you wearing all that palaver around your neck?" He removed hat and scarf to show he had completely cut his hair off.

I think he had a bit of a crush on me. Even when I got to Tshukudu he phoned me several times to ask if my husband was still alive. Although he seemed to be quite impressed with me I didn't take any notice of him, apart from treating him as a good friend.

Stewart married three or four times and the last time he came to visit us was on his so-called honeymoon. He was married to a wonderful woman – a baroness. Sadly, she died of cancer. But he really was a character.

Janusz also remembers Stewart, " He was the nicest guy. He had a fantastic personality but was the biggest storyteller I have ever met in my life. I worked out that if one believed all the things he claimed to have done in his life he would have been 250 years old! People loved him. He was strong and very well-built with a beard and women found him very attractive. When we were friends working together he won the Rhodesian lottery and I helped him spend it. We had holidays, boats, cars and women. I moved in with him in his cottage at Victoria Falls which he furnished with Persian rugs and other top-class stuff. When I left the money was gone. We had a mutual girlfriend. She was an artist's wife and Stewart introduced me to her and he lost her. He was quite bitter about it and I think that was why I left his house."

Back to what was happening in our home life: I was pregnant and had to think about what I would do so I started training a friend, Yvonne, to do the office work. She started a month before I gave birth to Ian and I used to pop in after he was born to see how she was managing. I blossomed when I was pregnant. My face was pretty but I was huge. I can remember driving, even though I was very heavily pregnant. We provided transport to pick up crews for Central African Airways. I recollect picking up the CAA guys at the Victoria Falls Hotel and seeing the grins on their faces when they saw who was behind the wheel, and watching the grins fade when they noticed the big stomach sticking up against the steering wheel. I enjoyed my pregnancy. I had very little morning sickness – only if I smelt coffee. I even went dancing. In fact, I went dancing the night before Ian was born!

All this time I had been trying to get my father out of Poland. It was very difficult. He was making every effort from his side and I was battling from the Livingstone end. Finally, I was able to send him a telegram saying we had managed to get him a Northern Rhodesia entry visa, and asking where I should send his ticket. He didn't need my ticket as he had saved enough himself and his telegram simply gave the date we could expect him at the airport. I was about seven months pregnant at the time. I told my mother and we just cried. We went into absolute hysteria. We didn't know where to start, what to organise, how to react. My mother had to fix up the flat. I was beside myself. I cannot express how I felt after not seeing my father for 18 years. I was a child of nine when I had said goodbye to him, hoping he would be back in a few days but not knowing if I would ever see him again. We decided that mum and dad should go up to the Victoria Falls so that they could get to know each other again.

When the plane arrived we were standing on the runway – pacing up and down not knowing what would happen. Then we saw people disembarking, and there he was. We were total strangers. I was grown up and pregnant and he remembered me as a child. When I saw Mother a few days later she said, "He's changed. Life has changed. It will never be the same again."

It was wonderful. Father loved fishing, so Lolly took him out on the river. All the time he and Mother had been separated, he had not had an affair. He loved Mother so much. He enjoyed riding his bicycle. It gave him pleasure to cycle down to the river. It was at about this time that Janusz and Ian, Lolly's brother, got up to all sorts of things.

In the middle of one very cold night in July, Janusz and Ian decided to go crocodile hunting. Of course they should not have been there and nobody knew what they were up to. The outboard motor, boat and guns were 'borrowed'. The river was in flood and the boat hit a log and went down fast. They managed to cling onto a small tree which was partly submerged. In Siberia Janusz discovered he had a mental gift for keeping himself warm even when it was freezing, but that night was really bad. They clung together to try to generate some heat. The guns had gone down with the boat so they had no defense against crocodiles. They knew that I did not know where they were and – even if I did – I couldn't go to

Ian and I

the police for help as they were intent on poaching.

When Janusz and Ian didn't return I nearly freaked out, especially as Odette, Ian's wife, was also pregnant. She didn't know what to do. I suggested we go out to look for them. I drove up and down the Katambora Road but didn't really know where to go. Eventually I said that we would just have to wait. I knew that if they had drowned we'd hear about it soon enough. They were eventually rescued, but had to do quite a bit of explaining about the 'borrowed' boat and Lolly's lost guns and engine.

My first child, Ian, was born on the day of Yvonne's birthday. Lolly went hunting that day. It was a Sunday, and my doctor, Corrie de Kock, had invited him to hunt on his farm. I went to have lunch with Mother and Father. Half an hour after lunch I felt the first pain. I thought, 'This is it.'

So I decided that I had better go home and prepare myself. Half an hour after I got home I felt another little niggle of pain so I got on the phone to Corrie and said, "There's nothing to panic about yet, but I would like my husband to come home. I'll let you know what's happening. At present the pains are about half an hour apart."

It took Lolly about an hour to get home by which time I had packed my bags. I told him that it was Yvonne's birthday party and I felt we should attend. So I got ready, had a cup of tea, rang Corrie to tell him to be at the hospital at about 6pm because I wanted to attend the party before I had the baby. By this time the pains were ten minutes apart, I felt that the party was important, even if we were only able to stay for a short time. We booked in at the hospital and went on to the party. At the party I ordered a sole but didn't really feel like eating it. Finally Lolly said, "I think we should go."

All my friends, including John Slade and Ken Momson, drove me to the hospital. At the hospital the nursing sister said, "Now stop playing funny games! Which one is the husband?"

They all denied it, including Lolly. I think he was so nervous. The nursing sister thought I was playing with her as I was kissing all the men goodbye at the door. Then they went off and I went in alone. I couldn't just lie there doing nothing, so the nurses got me to sort out the laundry and make them coffee until things got serious. Finally, Corrie came in and insisted that I had been pushing them around for long enough. When Ian was born all I could say was, "Oh heavens!" to which Corrie replied, "You're a long way from there!"

Corrie phoned Lolly in the middle of the night to tell him that the baby had Momson's hands, John Slade's hair and other parts from other men. It was such a happy, lovely atmosphere and the next morning at the office they all had champagne. All the guys hoped that the baby resembled them in some way.

Yvonne was running the office and I thought things were going well. I was very much in 'mother-mode' and enjoyed getting together with friends who also had babies so that we could compare notes. I divorced myself from the office, believing that my priority was my baby. I had some charming friends and being an at-home mother and housewife was fun – exactly what I needed at the time.

Nine months later I found I was pregnant again. It was very soon. I was not happy, partly because I was worried about the business and I didn't want to go through the birthing process again so soon.

The motel that we had purchased always had a la carte. We used to bring in entertainers, singers and strip-tease artists, and there were always men hanging around. Baby Ian had to get used to the noise. When I replaced the motel manager on his day off, Ian came with me in his carry cot. He also travelled with us from a very early age when we went fishing in Chobe. I never fussed about babies.

We bought a cottage in Serandellas on the Chobe River and going to Chobe was quite a thing. It was a long drive, usually towing a little boat. The house was on the other side of the river. We kept an old Ford truck on that side. When we crossed the river, Lolly would escort me from the boat and open the door of the Ford. I really thought that Lolly was developing into the perfect gentleman. However, once I was inside there was a rope to secure the door and stop me from falling out, which was really why he was being so polite. There were no brakes. I remember the 'Wenela' truck coming down the sandy road. The road was narrow and we had no brakes so we had to take off onto the side of the road. They were all very aware of our limousine! These trucks were the property of the recruiting company which operated in Kasane finding workers for their mines in South Africa.

A very old Scotsman, Pop Lamont, lived next door to our cottage. He fought on the side of the British against the Boers but he had become a real South African. He actually crossed sides during the war and fought against the English. After the war he worked on the mines in Barberton for a while. Then he worked as a ranger in the Kruger National Park. When he heard there were these cottages for sale in Serandellas he bought one and moved up there to retire.

Pop Lamont hated elephants because he had a mielie patch and the elephants used to come and flatten his crop. He didn't have a gun so he put down some dynamite and blew up an errant elephant. We arrived for a weekend and from several kilometres away we could smell the dreadful aroma of decaying elephant. The elephant was lying not far from our house and there were maggots all over it. These, however, didn't deter the local villagers who were busy cutting up the meat to take home to eat.

When I found out I was pregnant again, I left the running of the office to Yvonne. I had no problems at home as we lived very well in those days, the height of the colonial lifestyle. There was plenty of help at home. I had a cook, a gardener and someone who did the cleaning.

When I went into labour with my second baby it didn't really worry me. It was Good Friday and we were expecting family and friends for the Easter weekend. I went ahead and bought all the stuff that was needed and organised everything. The house was well stocked, and the servants capable of looking after it. I didn't think the pains were too serious. As it got closer to lunch time and our guests started to arrive, I said to Lolly, "I think you should drop me off at the hospital."

I also told the doctor that I didn't want to stay for the usual ten days, so four days after Chris was born I went home.

I started to notice that Lolly was always in a hurry to get away from home. He said that he needed to go to the motel. I suspected something was going on and I found out that Lolly was having an affair with Yvonne. I really liked Yvonne and had helped her and her three boys when their father had abandoned them, so I was

Mrs Mathews, Ian and Chris

naturally very upset that she was carrying on with my husband.

When Lolly got home I said, "Your father didn't want us to marry but we did. We've worked hard together to build up the business. You can't just mess everything up like this." I gave him an ultimatum. I said, "You have to make a decision. If you choose Yvonne please by all means go. But you can't have both of us. It's her or me."

I can be a very hard person and I think that in a situation when crucial decisions need to be made, I really show how hard I can be. Siberia comes out in me. So I said to him, "You are welcome to move in with her if that's what you want. The decision is yours, but if you decide to stay with me you will stop the affair with her this moment. I don't care what happens to the office. She'll have to leave tomorrow." The next morning I phoned her and told her to take everything that was hers and to leave the office. She had no excuse.

It was Odette, Lolly's sister-in-law, who persuaded me to stay with him. She stressed the need for a family to have both parents. I understood that many men are wanderers and that I had to accept it. I had the business and a beautiful life and I still loved Lolly. So I needed to just get on with it.

Fortunately, Chris was a very good baby. So I was able to return to the business. I have a business brain and Lolly is blessed with technical abilities. We had been a team. When I went back I was in for a shock. The business was in a mess. So I had to start from scratch.

The sad part about all this was that I had to go back to work when Chris was only three months old because of Lolly's indiscretion. I only had a couple of days in which to organise everything at home. Ian was probably a bit lost. It must have been a difficult time for him. I employed a Mrs Mathews to look after the boys. At the time I was unaware of the fact that she favoured Chris. Many years later someone told me about this. I loved my boys very much and I gave them all I could. It was not always easy – running a home as well as a business. But I still think that those two boys had the most wonderful life that any child could dream of. They often went boating with their father and they grew up with crocodiles in their home. Not only crocodiles but snakes and all kinds of creatures and goggas (insects). They had lots of love and many friends, and were constantly surrounded by kind people. Growing up in Livingstone was a fantastic experience for the boys. At that time it was a beautiful, wild and unspoilt area.

Livingstone was a small village and Ian still remembers trips to the islands over weekends, going waterskiing, swimming and fishing. He also remembers trips on the launch. As a child he can recall the house and describes it as a little place on the outskirts of the town with a garden, but most of all he remembers the freedom that he had to roam all over the place without any restrictions. He will never forget his first day at school and his friend, Andre Stapa, a young Anglo-Polish boy. It wasn't a good day for Ian. In fact, it was probably the biggest trauma in his little life, but his friend held onto him and said, "You mustn't be scared." He was a comfort in times of trouble and a great pal. Andre eventually moved to Harare (which was called Salisbury in those days). He joined the Air Force but when Rhodesia declared independence he moved over to the South African Air Force where he trained pilots to fight in the Angolan war. Sadly, many years later, Andre was reported missing in Angola. He was a fighter pilot and his plane had apparently been shot down. As an adult, Ian found this to be a very sad loss. I, too, cannot help remembering old friends.

Fire

We had three huge launches on the river, but usually used only two of them. One Sunday we had a lot of people which meant we needed an extra boat to accommodate them on the excursion. The one launch – seldom used – hadn't been taken out for a while and had a bit of history to it. We used to have sea planes from England landing on the Zambezi bringing tourists to view the Victoria Falls. When the flights came to an end, Lolly bought the boat that they had used for transporting passengers to and from the flying boats. The launch was extremely beautiful with a copper bottom and could hold 35 people.

On the particular day that we were to host the extra people, Lolly called me and said, "Please come and help me. I need to get the third boat on the go." I took the kids and rushed to the river. We went onto the boat and proceeded to clean and arrange seats. Somebody on the jetty called the children to come and look at a baby crocodile. The boys eagerly ran onto dry land to see this rarity. In the meantime, a friend of Lolly's, Van van Rensburg, tried to start the boat. He connected the battery and a spark shot out as he did. The boat had been standing for ages and was redolent with petrol fumes that had escaped from a leak in the petrol tank. The whole thing blew up! Flames shot into the air and fanned right across the surface of the boat, scorching everything or everyone in their path. It all happened so suddenly. There was no warning. I was at the front of the boat, so I was fortunate enough not to get the worst of it. Thank God the children had left the boat minutes earlier. Van had a badly burnt face, and my legs were burnt and bleeding but I was so shocked that I didn't immediately realise I was injured. Van and an assistant had to be rushed to hospital. The people arrived for their excursion and I went to meet them to apologise. Then I, too, was taken to emergency.

At the hospital they brought a wheelchair and I said, "No, I can walk," but suddenly I couldn't. It was so painful. I ended up spending ten days in hospital and the guys spent even longer.

The business flourishes

As an extension to our growing business Lolly took tour trips to the Wankie Game Reserve. At first there was no restaurant there, just camps. It was a really wonderful place – completely unspoiled. When there was a tour we would provide food for our guests. We had to take everything with us. Once we took a group that was to stay overnight, and the next day. The group members were mostly construction technicians from the Kariba Dam. They were not in the habit of eating dainty meals. Unaware of their appetites, I expected to be feeding people who were used to haute cuisine, and I planned the trip accordingly. I took ten loaves of bread for breakfast in the morning and some bread rolls for lunch. As a sign of events to follow, the hungry workers finished all ten loaves of bread at the evening meal. I had some tins of peaches for dessert, meant to feed the entire party. One guy took the whole dish of peaches, put it in front of himself and ate all of them! I couldn't believe it. I had never seen anything like it. So I had to open more peaches. They drank a lot of wine and didn't seem to mind if one took more food than the others. After this I became cunning, I started dishing out in small dishes. There were no shops in this place so I had to run around to the houses of the rangers begging for some bread in order to make toast for the morning meal.

Bruce Austin, who was in charge of the Wankie Game Reserve, invited a delegation of government ministers to visit the park. He needed more boreholes and other facilities, so he wanted the officials to come and do a needs assessment for themselves. He asked me to do the catering for the group. From this, the idea of a restaurant developed. I applied for the right to run the restaurant and this was the beginning of a new stage in our lives. We put two vehicles into the reserve and worked with Central African Airways and did all the groundwork for their flights into the reserve and organised the passengers. We were spreading our wings.

All the time we lived in Livingstone we were striving to move forward. We started the 'booze cruises', sundowner trips we ran on the Zambezi so people could see the spectacular sunsets while enjoying a drink. We wanted to have a bar on board to make the experience complete. Unfortunately there were a lot of old 'fuddy-duddies' on the Victoria Falls conservancy licencing committee and they turned down our application. In response to this we asked every passenger on our cruise to sign a petition. We succeeded in getting over a thousand signatures. Only one tourist refused to sign as drinking alcohol was against his religious beliefs. We submitted all the forms to the committee to show them what the tourists felt about being able to have a drink while on the cruise. The committee saw the light and granted us a licence. Now there are many licensed boats operating on the Zambezi River.

Central African Airways had the monopoly of flights into Livingstone. Another airline, Hunting Clan, wanted to come into the business but they just couldn't get off the ground. Ralf Miller, who was in charge of Hunting Clan in our area, came over to our house for dinner. He wanted to talk to us about introducing something different.

Ralf said, "I want to arrange for cheaper flights into Livingstone and I want you to put some excursions together that will work in conjunction with the flights. We could also ask some hotels to come on board with special rates and serve it all up as a packaged deal."

We put the whole thing together with Ralf, and our ideas started to sell. It took a long time to get off the ground but when it did it was a huge success. After the scheme had been running for some time Hunting Clan sold its licence to Central African Airways, which asked us to continue with the excursions that would be called 'Flame Lilly Holidays'. It grew from nothing to something very big and was born in our living room. It eventually had tours to Kenya, Tanganyika, Mozambique and South Africa.

We were also there when the Federation was formed between Nyasaland, Northern Rhodesia and Southern Rhodesia. It was fantastic because we could travel without passports and walk over to the Victoria Falls without going through customs. The unity did not last because the British Government was aiming to give independence to all of these countries. When the Federation broke up both Sir Roy Welensky and Ian Smith came to Livingstone and Lolly took the whole party for a boat trip on the Zambezi and there was a cocktail party and a banquet. We were involved in all of it. So we saw the birth and the death of the Federation.

By this time we had bought a travel agency from Sutherlands, we had a sporting shop, thirty vehicles, three launches on the Zambezi and the Falls Motel. We were growing at a tremendous speed. Lolly also did a lot of hunting which was lucrative but meant he would be away for as much as a month at a time, often with Janusz.

Janusz says goodbye to Livingstone

Janusz, who was still living in Livingstone, was always ingenious. He decided to build a houseboat. It was built like a floating platform with a thatch roof. Inside was a steel construction, but completely like a little house. It had a bar and a very big bed and was tastefully decorated. The boat was parked above the falls, and not too far away. To get to it one had to negotiate dangerous rapids so not many people went there on their own. We used to go there for parties or for lunches with lots of spaghetti, but it was Janusz's special place. We never slept there. The bed was exclusively for his use!

Some time after the houseboat had been built and put to use, Stewart Campbell approached Janusz with the story of a South African man who had been arrested in Lusaka for the rape of an under-age child. It was a trumped-up charge because the man was actually spying for South Africa. Stewart wanted to know if Janusz would be interested in getting him out of the country. Janusz drove to Lusaka, arriving very early in the morning. The man was under house arrest. Janusz devised a strategy to rescue him from his house and then managed to take him to the houseboat where he left him for three days until Stewart could organise with the South African government as well as the Rhodesian customs officials for Janusz to take him over the border into Rhodesia. For his efforts Janusz received the princely sum of five hundred pounds – a lot of money in those days.

While still discussing Livingstone, it is perhaps appropriate that I tell the story of Janusz's ignominious farewell to what was by then Zambia. With the change-over from Northern Rhodesia to an independent Zambia, all British flags had to be lowered and the new Zambian flag hoisted. Many celebrations were held to mark this memorable day. One such flag was hoisted at the local Police Station. In a fit of loyalty towards the old regime (or perhaps it was just cussedness), Janusz lowered the Zambian flag at the Police Station and hoisted the Union Jack. Of course the dreadful deed was perpetrated at the dead of night. Kenneth Kaunda was greatly displeased and made a statement on the radio that if he caught the person responsible for dishonouring the new national symbol they would do the same to him. Janusz had told too many people about what he had done, and quite a few of those people would have been happy to see him dangling from a flag pole so he packed his things into his convertible and drove to Johannesburg. However, he had left a fairly large sum of money behind in a Livingstone bank and he needed the money. So about a month later he decided to return to collect it.

Ala's Story

On reaching customs on the Zambian side of the border post it was apparent to Janusz that they were looking for him. When they took his passport and slipped it under the counter he knew he was in trouble. Anyway, they allowed him into Zambia without his passport and said they would return it when he again went through Immigration on his return trip. He contacted a girlfriend who worked in the bank. She managed to access the money. He then phoned a friend living on the Southern Rhodesian side of the border at Victoria Falls and asked if he would help to retrieve the passport. The plan was that while Janusz was trying to get through the border on the Zambian side, his friend would sneak behind the counter and retrieve the passport from under the counter where Janusz had seen them put it. He was banking on the usual inefficiency of those working at the post and that they had not done anything about his entry. When he asked for his passport at the Zambian counter it was obvious that they had not taken any action. With a sense of urgency – even panic – they immediately tried to reach the police. Janusz began shouting and performing and attracted attention to himself so that his friend was able to sneak into the office and get the troublesome document. Fortunately, the officials had neglected to stamp the passport when they had initially confiscated it. Once he was sure that it was safely in the hands of his friend, Janusz stormed out of Immigration and returned to Livingstone. From there he went by boat across to Victoria Falls where his friend was waiting with the passport. Southern Rhodesian officials were also waiting for him. They asked if he had been to Livingstone which he denied. They examined his passport which had no stamp so, although they guessed he had crossed the border, they could prove nothing. After that he lived in Johannesburg.

Janusz was then made a prohibited immigrant and could not return to Zambia so I bought the houseboat from him. Some time later we were accused of sending signals to Rhodesia from the boat which was a lot of nonsense – just a political trumped-up thing. I think I gave the boat to someone just before we, too, left Livingstone.

Reflections

We knew such a lot of characters in Livingstone. They were wonderful people but some gave me a lot of trouble. I tried to educate them to save money and to teach them to live a decent life but it never worked out as I planned. We lived in Livingstone for 18 years, but after the break-up of the Federation we felt that the time had come to move on.

Thinking back on our time in Livingstone, I often wonder how this brother of mine felt about his mother and me when he got up to all his nonsense. He always claims that he loved his family very much, and that he still remembers all the things we went through. To him Mother was an angel, but he felt that I had treated him like a little boy all his life. Mother did not always know what he was up to, I shielded her. Only in later years did Janusz express regrets about the things he should have done for his parents.

"I have hurt my family. I have hurt women and in later years, I have hurt myself. But that was life. I was silly," admits Janusz.

I really think my children had a stable life as little boys in Livingstone. They didn't go for radios and music but they had great times on the launches – water skiing and taking part in all the activities and they enjoyed the comfort and luxury of a typical colonial lifestyle.

The children also brought great joy to my father's life. He took great pleasure in his grandchildren. Once we went to the circus. The children were absolutely beside themselves – laughing and giggling, especially at the chimpanzee. Father didn't watch the circus acts, his eyes only took in the enjoyment and enthusiasm of the children. He also grew to love Africa. When he first came to Livingstone he couldn't speak English so in order to try to improve his English I gave him lessons in the afternoons. I have so many regrets. I should have done more for him.

One day when I went to visit Father he was uncomfortable and complained of heartburn. The pain persisted so I called the doctor who came to see him. The doctor said it looked serious so I made arrangements for an afternoon charter flight to take Tatus to Bulawayo – the nearest modern medical facility – and the doctor suggested he rest quietly until then. At lunch time Mother came to my house. She did not say anything, but I knew. I went back to their house and there I found what I had been dreading – my Tatus had passed away. It was terribly sad. We only had four years together after the eighteen years of separation. We buried him in Livingstone. Years later we went back to try to trace his grave but, sadly, they have buried other people on top of where his grave should have been. We found the plaque lying in the middle of a road. His bones must stay there and my mother's would eventually be laid to rest in Nelspruit, but their spirits will be with

Ala's Story

us always. One is so busy with one's own life. We have regrets but we would do the same again. We should be spending more time with our families. I did spend half an hour each day with Father, but that was very little. One thing I remember: when he was with his grandchildren he was a very happy person. I suppose I was really lucky. Many people don't even have four years together.

When we are young we reach for happiness. We all do, and we all strive to reach the top. But when you grow up and get older you are sensible and you think back on life and you will always have regrets. I also have regrets about my mother. I could have done so much more for her. Now I appreciate what she did for me. As a child you are selfish and don't think about others. When you get married and you're building your life you don't seem to have time to think much about your parents. Today, being older, I know what she went through. I think every person has some kind of regrets in their lives, things they would probably like to correct.

Part 3
A Lodge in Chobe
1963 - 1980

Goodbye to
Livingstone

Before we left Livingstone we used to visit Chobe for weekend breaks. We had
a little cottage in Serandellas and loved the wild beauty of the place. Originally,
the group of five riverside cottages belonged to Serandellas Sawmills. When
the cottages were later put up for sale we were lucky enough to buy one. One
weekend, on the way to our cottage, we stopped at the Chobe Hotel for a drink.
Bechuanaland Protectorate, or Botswana as it's now called, wasn't particularly
geared for tourism at this time and the hotel at Chobe was an oasis in this vast,
untamed land. Chobe Hotel had been built by Charles and Ethnee Holmes à Court.
They set the enterprise in motion from a humble caravan on the banks of the
Chobe River and, with great determination, they built the hotel. This became the
only tourist operation in the area for quite some time. On one of their first safaris
Mr Holmes à Court was taking two ladies from Cape Town on a fishing trip when
they were attacked by a swarm of bees. One of the ladies panicked and shouted,
"Oh my God! I'm allergic to bees!"

   In an attempt to save the ladies, Charles shouted for them to dive into the river,
crocodiles and all. Unfortunately by the time he took to the water he had already
been badly stung, and emerged from the river looking like a swollen sack. He was
rushed to hospital in Bulawayo but didn't survive. Ethnee Holmes à Court was left
to manage on her own in the bush. There were no decent roads leading in or out,
so she was pretty isolated. I really admired them for what they had built and for
her courage in carrying on after the death of her husband. She had two sons. At
the time we met, one of them was living in Australia, the other died tragically and
very mysteriously in the Tsitsikama forest, in the Cape, some time later. Her eldest
son came to visit her when they first started the business, but couldn't imagine
a life for himself living in the isolated bush so he moved to Australia where
he became a lawyer and ended up as Australia's first billionaire and one of its
wealthiest men. He even owned an island and started breeding race horses. Ethnee
eventually joined her son in Australia. I believe she still, at the age of more than
90, lives in Perth (at the time of writing this book).

   On this particular weekend on our way to Chobe we were greeted by a
distraught Ethnee. She had been trying to sell the hotel and thought she had a
prospective buyer but she thought the deal had fallen through. "Lolly, Lolly,"
she cried when she saw us, "I've got to sell this place. I have a ticket to fly to
Australia to live with my son, and the guy who was supposed to buy the hotel has

reneged on the sale. Please won't you buy it?"

Lolly's rather surprised response was, "No, what do we want to buy a hotel for?"

Jokingly we said, "We're with friends now. Why don't you visit us tomorrow morning when we can talk about it." As our cottage was only about 12km away this was not a totally unreasonable request.

Next morning there was a knock on the door and there stood Ethnee with her lawyer. She said, "I've come in the hope that we can persuade you to buy my hotel."

Lolly and I looked at each other and, on the spur of the moment, we agreed. We had no idea what we were getting ourselves into. We felt that, as always, God had a plan for our lives. So we went ahead with the deal.

On our return to Livingstone we approached Lolly's mom who was visiting us from Lusaka, and asked her to help out until we appointed a manager.

"Mom, we want you to take stock at the Chobe place, and then to take over the running of it so that we have time to make future plans."

We had bought the hotel not knowing that things were deteriorating in Northern Rhodesia, and that we would need a safe haven to fly to. How fortuitous that when we needed it we did have a place to go.

I had been attending a travel agent's course in Salisbury prior to our going to Chobe for the weekend, and returned to complete the course there after we got back to Livingstone. On arriving home again I was met by Lolly who said that half of Livingstone had left because trouble was brewing. He felt that we should also be making plans to get out while we could. That's when I sent a telegram.

For some time now a company called United Touring Company, part of British Transport, had been nibbling at our business and making proposals to buy. Up to this point in time we'd had no interest in selling. This company specialised in upmarket tours in Kenya and other African countries. In fact, they offered tours in many different parts of the world.

My telegram to them simply said, "Business for sale!" I immediately received a reply, "Arriving in three day's time."

The company had already bought out a business in Salisbury called 'Overland Tours' and was eager for the previous owner of this tourist-based venture, Willy Seeman, to run it, as well as our enterprises. The United Touring Company asked me to stay on for a year to manage the Livingstone, Victoria Falls and Wankie Game Reserve branches, with the result that Lolly had to go to Chobe on his own. Unfortunately, I did not see eye-to-eye with Mr Seeman. He tried to impose his methods of running the business, contrary to many of the tried and tested ideas that we had used. Our business was successful, and I didn't see the logic of his changing our practices. He put up the prices and interfered so much that I really wasn't happy.

I phoned him and said, "I cannot bear working with you any more, I want to get out."

I got hold of London and said, "I really want to leave. I know I signed for a year, but I've had enough although it's only been six months."

They asked me to train somebody else which I did. We had an amicable dinner at the Victoria Falls Hotel and parted company. I left for Chobe. We re-named Chobe Hotel to Chobe Safari Lodge, which still exists and has since grown into an enormous success.

Life at the lodge

One of the big problems that we faced was our sons' education. Before we moved to Chobe they attended a convent in Livingstone. When I also left Livingstone we decided that they should stay with my mother and finish off their school year where they were. Ian remembers this as a good time – being spoilt by a loving grandmother. I left in May and they stayed until December. They were still quite small. Chris was six and Ian was eighteen months older.

At Chobe there was a heap of work, a lot of finishing off to do. Ethnee and her husband had beautiful ideas. There were eight guest rooms in the hotel, all overlooking the Chobe River. It was an incredibly lovely place, heaven on earth. Now it's changed. It's become overcrowded and over-run by tourists. Nowadays if there is a lion kill people flock to see it, with masses of cars lining up to get that special photograph that will make them famous. We have been back, but it lacked the old excitement for me.

Once we really got working at the lodge the business started to take off. We had many contacts through Flame Lily Holidays and I quickly got the Chobe experience booked into that. I brought a lot of travel agents from South Africa to introduce them to this paradise, and it worked.

Our lodge in Chobe

Ala's Story

We had our share of teething troubles. After Ethnee left, Lolly's mother took over and we then hired a Polish guy as the manager. Unfortunately, he wasn't suited for the demanding job. We were not only running the hotel, but we also had three trading stores. One was in Kasane itself, one at Panda Matanga and one at Kachikau, then a little village on the way to Katimo Molilo. We also ran a ferry-cum-pontoon crossing between Zambia and Bechuanaland. Among many others, our clientele included the South African policemen from Katimo Mulilo on the other side of the river and all the passing trade. Transport for Victoria Falls had to come past Chobe, and the drivers usually stopped off for a drink. At times the border posts would be closed and we would have to accommodate drivers and travellers for a night. I can remember some of them sleeping in the lounges or wherever we could find place.

There was a huge baobab tree nearby which was of historical significance. It was the meeting place of four countries. Northern Rhodesia was just across the river, and it was also the border for Bechuanaland, Southern Rhodesia and the Caprivi Strip (South Africa). Legend has it that David Livingstone had actually camped under this very tree.

Politically, things were never boring. It was like living in a John Le Carré novel, full of international intrigue. Before Southern Rhodesia became Zimbabwe there was a lot of animosity between it and Zambia, so we had the airforcemen and spies coming from Zambia and they would drink in our pub; we had Southern Rhodesians coming on 'fishing' trips, and South African guys also trying to get information. They would all meet in the pub trying to find out what was going on across the river. The only way they could get over the river was on the pontoon. It was an interesting melting pot. We had some great nights in our pub!

The lodge was in the village of Kasane. It was a beautiful spot – totally unspoiled. On game drives the only vehicle was Lolly's and there was just so much game – herds of elephant and buffalo, prides of lions and beautiful buck which are unique to that area, the Sititunga, the Puku, and the Chobe bushbuck – although not all of these were in our immediate area. People would come from everywhere just to see the buck and also the huge herds of elephant crossing the river which one could view from the verandah of the lodge. Lolly was very knowledgeable about the elephants, but he was also naughty.

"I was the only one who drove tourists to see the animals in those days," says Lolly. "One day I drove a tourist group into the middle of a herd of elephants and then switched off the vehicle's ignition. A lady turned around and saw an elephant pushing at the back of the car. She fainted, so I threw a bag of water over her. When she came round she wanted to know why I had done that because she had recently done her hair!" Another time when they were surrounded by elephants Lolly felt a wallet fall into his lap.

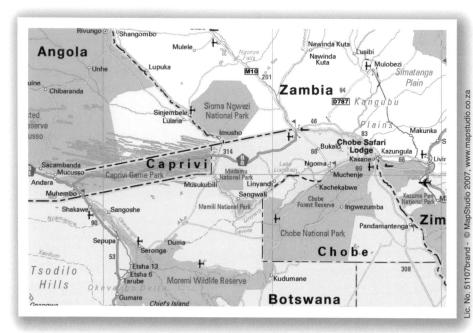

A recent map of the Chobe area showing the meeting point of four countries: Zambia, Zimbabwe, Botswana and the formerly SA-controlled Caprivi Strip

"Please just go!" said a timid voice. So they went. (Lolly did return the wallet with its contents intact!). Lolly had no fear of the animals. Fortunately no one ever got hurt.

Once, he took Chris with him on one of his excursions. Chris must have been about six years old, the vehicle slewed into an elephant spoor and overturned. Chris was thrown (or perhaps jumped) to safety. No one was injured and they were able to right the vehicle. They had taken flasks of tea with them so they sat around drinking tea to calm their nerves. They perched Chris on the roof of the vehicle. He was rather pleased with himself and kept saying, "Dad, I'm nearly dead."

On their way back to the Lodge they found two buffalo covered in blood. They went a little further and found a lion that had been killed by the buffalo and another that was badly wounded. On their return they immediately informed Pat Hepburn, the game warden, about the wounded lion. He found the injured animal and put it out of its misery but there was no trace of the buffalo. The following day he brought the two lion skins to us. We urged him to keep the skins as evidence of the shooting.

The boys spent time with us at Chobe during their school holidays while they

Ala's Story

were still at school in Livingstone. The adventurous life and the freedom there made them want to make it permanent. Once they had completed their year at the convent, they joined us at Chobe for good. Anne Hutchinson, an American girl, had come looking for a job while they were still away in Livingstone. I asked her what her profession was, and she said she had trained as a teacher. Not really thinking about my own sons, I said that I was sorry but had no opening for her. She then went off to Salisbury where she got an appointment as a teacher at Kariba. About a month or two later, when I was desperate about schooling for the boys, it suddenly dawned on me that I had let a good teacher slip through my fingers. I traced Anne from Salisbury to Kariba. I offered her a job to home school my two boys. Fortunately she was able to join us and began to tutor them in the Rhodesian correspondence course.

Chris and Ian always thought that these were the finest years of their lives. This was the best 'school' they ever attended, and they were able to travel all over with us because we could take their teacher along. We went on holiday to South West Africa (now known as Namibia), and travelled all around Bechuanaland. When Janusz visited us at Chobe, it was declared a school holiday. In fact, if anything exciting happened school would come to a standstill. Like the time when important guests arrived or when the horse fell into the swimming pool.

Our alcoholic horse, Gypsy, was a good reason for bringing lessons to a standstill. His penchant for a stiff drink would entice him up to the compound where he would knock the top off a 44-gallon (200 litre) drum and consume its home brew contents. He would drink and drink until he was on his knees. In a state of total inebriation he had difficulty in walking back to the Lodge. When he reached the gate he would sway from pole to pole in order to negotiate it. Often he would walk to the front of the Lodge and, in his sozzled state, tended to fall into the swimming pool which caused a huge commotion whenever we tried to get him out. Everyone would come to give advice or assistance. Once rescued he would be carted off to the police station where the policemen had built a special compound to hold him until he had sobered up. We would have to go to bail him out.

Gypsy was also not too keen on strangers riding him. He would tolerate Chris, Ian and Sandra Haylock, who was with her parents Tony and Mavis who were making a film about wild animals, but no one else could ride him. On one occasion a rough character by the name of 'Tiger', who was staying at the Lodge, asked if he could go riding. I told him that the horse was extremely difficult to control and it liked to throw riders. I really did not want him to break his neck. The brash reply was, "Oh! I know how to handle horses!"

Gypsy was so clever! We used to have a pit for broken bottles that were non-returnable. For safety reasons this pit was a fair distance from the Lodge. The intrepid Tiger mounted Gypsy. Initially the horse bucked and spun in an unsuccessful effort to unseat its rider. Finally he seemed to accept the load and Tiger relaxed thinking he had won the battle. Just as they were passing the bottle pit Gypsy reared up then kicked his hind legs and off flew Tiger right into the pit of broken bottles. He limped back to the Lodge clutching the seat of his pants.

Chris remembers another ploy that Gypsy used. He would appear docile and allow people to mount and ride him. He would take them for a long ride towards the border post, a distance of about twelve kilometres. He would behave himself beautifully all the way there but as they approached the fence he would take off and brake suddenly, throw the victim unceremoniously to the ground, then turn around and gallop home riderless. We would later find the disconsolate riders slowly trudging back along the road vowing never to ride again.

There was no end to the schemes of this wily horse. He tried anything to unseat riders. He would gallop, lickety split, down the slope towards a huge trellis which stood near the lodge, stop suddenly and try to forge a union between rider and rambling roses – a painful and thorny experience for the recipient. Being thrown off a horse into a trellis would be something he might not want to tell his friends at home about. Gypsy managed this on several occasions. What an amazing horse! One day some visitors had arrived in a very elegant car. It had leather upholstery which was quite posh in those days. They left the car windows open so that the smell of their padkos (food for the journey), which they left in the car, would not permeate the expensive interior. The car was close to the tennis courts where we kept a drum filled with molasses, which was used to help maintain the tennis court. Gypsy found the drum and, having an incredibly sweet tooth, proceeded to spoon it out with his tongue. Then he became aware of the enticing food smells emanating from the car. With sticky molasses dribbling from his mouth, he sauntered over to the parking lot and helped himself through the open car window. All that beautiful white leather covered in sticky molasses!

Ian helped out by taking guests on the river fishing as well as sightseeing. This would occur when Lolly was too busy or perhaps not well. He was only eight at the time, so he had to take one of the local guides along so as to have an adult on board. Ian did all the driving. On one occasion (actually I think that Lolly was with him at that time) a hippo bit the propeller of the boat off and on another a hippo bit the side of the boat. Fortunately it did not overturn.

Kasane now has about 20 to 30 lodges. When we lived there most of its residents worked for the police, the government or for us. Now it's a sprawling town.

There were so few other people when we lived there so it felt that the river belonged to us. And there weren't public roads so even the vast Game Park felt as if it was ours alone! Lolly was the only one taking tours into it.

"Because of dad's crocodile hunting days in Livingstone he knew the river well

Ala's Story

and we also got to know how to handle ourselves on it and how to go down the rapids where the Chobe and the Zambezi met." Ian continues to reminisce. "The fishing was unbelievable. One day Chris and I went out with our cousin and we caught 101 fish in one hour. Our boat was a big 'bag' full of fish. It was idyllic."

Fishing was a great attraction for visitors. The abundant shoals of tiger fish and bream meant that even a novice went away with the thrill of landing a catch.

Lolly opened up the first safaris to Savuti which is between Kasane and Maun – south of where we lived. The Savuti River came out of the Kwando River and flowed into the Savuti swamps. At that time it was estimated that it had one of the largest concentrations of wild life in Africa. The Savuti River was a beautiful crystal clear flow of water and had massive trees in it that must have been about fifty years old. The river had apparently stopped flowing a long time ago and the trees grew where the river had once been. Then the rains came and the river ran again. All the trees were now in the river. Lolly opened up roads in the Savuti. It was actually part of the Chobe National Park.

Ian remembers an incident on the Savuti, "One day a chap was going up the river in a boat and he hit a submerged tree stump and lost his propeller. Because of the scarcity of spares, we went up the river and tried to find the propeller by walking in the water. While moving around in the water a hippo emerged between us and the boat, so we had to do some fairly rapid water-walking to get to safety. Sometime later this same chap was actually bitten by a hippo and had to spend a few months in hospital. Some people do take foolish risks!"

During the annual rains the Zambezi and Chobe rivers would flood the land in front of our lodge. Villages would be under water and daring rescues had to be carried out. Once, when the flood was unexpected, Lolly and Pop Lamont had to ferry about 500 people out of water-logged villages to Serandellas. The lodge itself was always safe from flooding because it had been built on a high bank above the water line. The raging waters disturbed much of the wildlife and many different species of animals could be seen swimming across the swollen river trying to reach the safety of higher ground. We saw huge crocodiles in the surging waters. It was also not unusual to see huge mambas (very poisonous snakes) battling against the river currents. They would often take refuge in trees, but were forced down to search for food and ended up in the water. During this time we had a particularly bad time with the black mambas. We tried to shoot them as we saw them swimming towards us because the bite of a mamba is lethal and we were fearful for the lives of the people camping near the water.

When the rivers were flooded and the snakes were washed off the Caprivi Strip and tried to swim to the mainland, the boys would follow them in their boat and shoot as many as they could. One day Chris came back to the Lodge with a huge mamba that he'd shot with his pellet gun. The gun was not particularly powerful so the pellets only penetrated half way. The snake was weighed down with all the pellets, but was really only unconscious. It is amazing that he was never bitten. The good Lord was looking after them. People wondered why I allowed my sons to take a rod and a rifle and disappear on their little boat down the river, but I couldn't keep them chained up. I knew where they were, although sometimes I did not know what they were up to!

Because of the wild nature of the area and, of course, the floods, there were several other incidents involving snakes, especially mambas. At the back of our bedroom there was a mosquito net which covered a verandah. One day a staff member came running in to us and said, "There's a mamba inside."

All the men were away so I ran to the bar to see who was there. There were two Englishmen. I asked if either could shoot and I explained about the snake. It was obvious that neither had ever held a gun so I phoned the police who said, "Sorry, the captain is away and we do not have a gun."

Then it struck me – Chris had sold his pellet gun to our chef. I rushed to the kitchen and asked, "Lamson, can you shoot?"

When he replied in the affirmative, I asked if he would be able to kill a snake. He said that he didn't have any bullets for the gun. I found some pellets in Chris's bedroom.

The mamba was huge. It had slithered into a corner. Lamson shot it over and over and over again. The pellets were small and did not seem to make much of an impact. Eventually its head was so full of pellets that it was too heavy to lift and so was relatively harmless and could be taken outside to be disposed of.

Another time I was picking up my washing from the floor and it seemed to be heavier than usual. Curled up in the dirty laundry was another mamba – that was a close shave!

The fear of mambas was a very legitimate one. Chris recalls one evening when friends had come to join us for a *braai* (barbeque). Quite late in the evening a lady decided she was going to put the children to bed so she went into the bedroom with the kids. She put her hand under the bed in order to get some clothes out of a suitcase and felt something slimy and cold – it was a huge black mamba. She called the children to come out of the bedroom and they ran to us in a panic. The adults, especially the men, had been hitting the booze and were all a little under the weather. They all went into the lady's room to kill the snake. They were armed with kettles of boiling water, bricks, stones and anything else they could lay their hands on. They trashed the room completely trying to kill the snake in their drunken state. Meantime, the snake curled up in a drawer. The men then completely pulverised the chest of drawers. The wily snake, in an effort to escape these death-wielding attackers, slithered up into the rafters. By this time it was quite badly injured, and running for its life. Chris ran back to the Lodge and got

Ala's Story

his pellet gun. He proceeded to put about 20 to 30 pellets into the snake, which finally gave up the fight and fell down, dead.

Nearly getting killed was a regular occurrence for the boys. The Chobe River was infested with crocodiles and they really did stupid things. They skied and swam in the river, but did so with great caution. I now wonder how they survived. They were growing up in a potentially dangerous environment but, like living in a big city and being aware of the dangers of heavy traffic, they had to learn how to be safe in the bush. They knew the river backwards and never seemed to have any fears or reservations about their adventures. They did not think that they were taking unnecessary risks. As they were growing up, I insisted that they should be home at certain hours but felt that I could not restrict their movements. They had been given a special opportunity and I could not impose limits.

Ian reckons that they must have had a whole army of guardian angels. They were small boys accompanied by an equally small fox terrier and anything small is regarded as a target for wild animals. They deemed the whole area, including the rivers, as their back yard. It was an unbelievable lifestyle. They had the freedom of the vast uninhabited bush – a place where the seeds of their future were planted.

Major Lamb and a guest in our bar

While we were establishing the lodge, we entrusted our fully furnished house in Serandallas to a caretaker by the strange name of 'Cockeye'. He certainly had an eye for opportunity. When he saw how successful our lodge in Kasane was becoming he decided to begin an enterprise of his own. He owned a mokoro and started to ferry terrorists from the Caprivi Strip across the river and then accommodate them in our house – in our beds! They paid him in English pounds. Cockeye spent his money at a trading store owned by a Greek gentleman by the name of Mr Louzides who became suspicious as to the source of the English money and enquired where Cockeye was getting it from. The reply was anything but satisfactory. We asked the local policemen to check on our property in case Cockeye was stealing from it or something. The policemen discovered the ferrying and accommodation business. They also discovered that the resourceful Cockeye had been poaching for meat to feed his guests. For his troubles he received six months in jail. On being released in January he visited us at the lodge and told us that he had come to collect his Christmas present!

The accommodation at the Lodge consisted of six rooms, twelve rondawels and two family cottages. There were also often campers. We never knew exactly how many people we would have at any one time. Some days we would have two people booked in at the lodge but by the end of the evening the number could swell to as many as 20 guests. Sometimes people were so taken by the beauty of the place that they could not resist delaying their departure and spending an extra night there. I used to keep a supply of bully beef in our shop in Kasane and there was always fresh bream (fish). This proved to be popular with the guests. One man said he could eat bream for breakfast, lunch and dinner.

One day, while driving our truck to Kachikau, I met Dick from Wenella, a mining recruitment company. He was in charge of the Katimo Mulilo part of the business, and stopped his truck to have a chat. He introduced me to a lady seated next to him. I didn't recognise her but we chatted for a while and I said that I was on my way to Kachikau. The next day I received a radio message to say that the lady I had met was from Springbok Radio in South Africa where she ran a woman's programme and would I please accommodate her and be interviewed? In the interview she asked me how I managed to get provisions, how I prepared the food and how I, as a woman, coped with life in this wild country. I said that one gets so used to it that you learn to improvise.

"If you run out of some of the ingredients for bread, you make *vetkoek*." (Vetkoek is dough with yeast, fried in oil or fat).

Many new visitors came as a result of the programme. We even made friends with people from Nelspruit in South Africa who visited us there after hearing the interview on the radio – and they've remained friends to this day.

Getting good staff in Chobe was not easy. I had to train them myself. Our chef was from Northern Rhodesia, so he had to have his special permit to stay renewed every six months. Ironically, it was over weekends, when we were busiest, that the staff would cut loose with the most raucous parties.

Lolly was the General Manager of all the maintenance, water sources and the generators. I ran the lodge and each day at Chobe was very busy. In order to complete all my tasks I would have to get up at 5am and send out the early morning tea trays to the visitors in their rooms. Then I would supervise breakfast. Once that was over we would start baking biscuits and cakes for tea. I would then order supplies – petrol, produce and any other things that we needed, then deliver the petrol and do so many other chores. Our supplies came by train from Bulawayo to Victoria Falls, then by truck on practically non-existent roads for 40 miles. This was far from adequate but it had to do and everything came this way, from bread to beer, asparagus to alcohol. Even our ice-cream was packaged in special boxes and transported from Bulawayo. I did have a cold room but limited space in the deep freezer so it was quite an art to order everything we needed, then get supplies on time and make sure we had sufficient space in which to keep the food fresh. I was responsible for the pontoon and also ran the Botswana Airways agency and sometimes even had to chase animals off the runways when the planes wanted to land. We also acquired a twin-engine plane, and employed a pilot, for charter flights and private use. My days were so hectic that there seemed to be no time for anything else.

Independance comes to Bechuanaland

There was great excitement in Bechuanaland. It was to receive its independence. Princess Marina, Duchess of Kent, flew from England to do the honours on behalf of Great Britain and she was to spend some time at our lodge. Major Lamb was our district commissioner and we had a small celebration in Kasane when the British flag was lowered and the new flag hoisted. Bechuanaland was to be known as Botswana.

About a week before Princess Marina arrived, 'terrorists' were discovered in the area. In Kazangula which was about ten kilometres away from the lodge, six men went into the shop and bought food. Being a small community where everyone knows everyone else, six strangers buying food was cause for gossip and the shopkeeper told anyone who cared to listen about them and where they said they were going. They were headed for a River-Bushman village a little further up towards the Rhodesian side. Two stalwart policemen on bicycles went up to investigate. These terrorists were armed with AK-47s! Everybody thought it was

Major Lamb at the flag-raising ceremony

a huge joke that two policemen on bicycles arrested six 'terrorists' armed to the teeth. After the terrorist scare we had CID everywhere. The royal visit was nearly cancelled as they were fearful for the safety of the princess but eventually she came. One of the reasons for her visit was that Sir Seretse Khama, the head of state in Botswana, loved Chobe. Seretse, his wife Ruth, and their children used to regularly come and stay in the Game Department Camp. They spent a lot of time tiger fishing with Lolly. I remember one day when they were visiting, Lolly had malaria and was feeling pretty ill. Seretse was determined to have his fishing trip, but would not go with just anyone.

"I'm not going on the river unless Lolly takes me," he said. So I told Lolly, "You can die tomorrow, but today you will go fishing."

We had to be trained how to behave in the presence of royalty. We were not allowed to address the princess unless she spoke to us first, and we were told not to call her 'your highness' she preferred to be called 'Ma'am'.

In preparation for the visit my mother had decorated the lodge with about 27 bouquets of flowers picked from the bush. The decor was enhanced by bushmans' animal skins that were laid throughout the lodge. Lolly drove my lovely convertible to Serrandellas to fetch the royal party. Princess Marina and Major Lamb sat in the back while Lolly acted as chauffeur.

Lolly was scheduled to take her on a boat trip, and they were to be accompanied by a security boat that would follow them. Lolly escorted Princess Marina to the jetty where they were to meet the guards. They waited and waited for the security boat to arrive but it didn't appear. Lolly knew he wasn't supposed to go without it, but he got impatient and said to Marina, "Sweetie, what are we waiting for? Let's go!" They got onto the boat and off they went. Apparently the security boat had experienced trouble getting its motor started. When they eventually got to the jetty they were understandably curious as to where Princess Marina was. All we could tell them was, "They've gone." So they had to chase after Lolly. Lolly was in deep water!

I had organised a special dining room for the royal guests so they wouldn't have to sit with the other people. Princess Marina sent me a message saying that in no way should anyone be put out by her visit and that she wanted to join all the other guests for meals. There was also a cocktail party in her honour at the lodge. When she spoke to me I asked her if she had enjoyed her dinner she replied, "It was the best meal I've had in Botswana."

That night I saw her leave her room and go to her maid of honour and then return to her own room. The next moment the maid of honour came rushing out, complete with curlers in her hair, and said, "There's a spider in Princess Marina's bathroom."

The detectives wanted to go to the rescue but I stopped them and said that

HRH Princess Marina, accompanied by Major Lamb, being welcomed to our Chobe lodge by the Police Chief's daughter, a staff member's daughter and me

they should wait for Lolly. I was scared that they would start smashing walls or windows in their attempts to kill the spider. Lolly came downstairs and carefully removed the spider. The following day we were summoned to her room. She congratulated us on our wedding anniversary and apologised for her panic over the spider, but explained that she was not used to having them in her bedroom in England. She was such a lovely person. She signed a photograph and on it wrote, "This day will be memorable."

About six months after their visit Seretse and Ruth were invited to dinner at Princess Marina's royal house in England. Over dinner they discussed the trip to Botswana. Ruth asked her what she had enjoyed the most, what were her most memorable moments? She said, "I will never forget Chobe. I was called 'sweetie' for the first time in my life."

Unfortunately she died of a brain tumor a year later.

About 12 to 15 years ago Sir Seretse's son, Ian, was at the Maun airport taking a salute for his army and we were sitting on the bench waiting for our flight. Ian Khama came over to us and greeted us. He remembered us although he was only a young lad when he had visited Chobe. His action underlined the really good relationship that existed between us and his father.

Janusz remembers his visits to Chobe. He reckons that he must have courted every white woman there. Normally I welcomed his visits but after one particular incident I really felt that he should not come again.

We had a policeman, Des, who was married to Jennifer. We were very dependent on Des for all our licences and permits so we needed to keep him sweet. Once, when Janusz was staying with us, someone asked me if I knew that he was leaving that night and would not be going alone but with Jennifer. I had to act quickly. I phoned the customs and immigration on the Botswana side as well as on the Rhodesian side of the border and I said, "Please don't let my brother through the border."

I knew all the officials pretty well and so was able to spoil his fun for a little while. He left later, but by himself. One day Lolly and I had to go to Bulawayo on business and Jennifer asked if she could get a lift because she had to see a gynaecologist. I cleared it with Des before agreeing to let her come along. He was fed up with the whole story, and said that he didn't think it really mattered whether she went or not. So we took her and she caught the first train out of Bulawayo to Johannesburg to stay with Janusz. She later went to the Vaal River and stayed with a friend of mine. I don't think her romance with Janusz lasted very long.

The worst thing about this story is that it disrupted so many lives. Des eventually ended up with the Warden's wife, Mary Hepburn.

Ours was a small community. There was Major Lamb who would pop into the bar each morning for his pink gin and then go back to the office. Then there was Captain Webb who we had known from our Livingstone days. We were determined to play cupid and match him up with a partner. Once, when there was a police ball in Livingstone and Lolly was ill and we were unable to go, Webby suggested that I should go with him as his partner. I didn't think this would be a good idea so I organised that he take Ruth, a friend of mine. The next day when I asked him how he had enjoyed the dance he replied, "I am going to marry that woman!" They eventually tied the knot and came to live in Kasane. He did, however, have one weakness – he used to enjoy listening into conversations on our party-line telephone.

Of course, there were times when I didn't want anybody listening to my conversations. One such call involved my trying to obtain petrol. Getting petrol was a huge problem. After independence we were without it for two months. We simply had to exist without it, but we needed fuel to run the generator and to keep the boats going. Obviously the boats were a main source of income. The difficulty arose from the animosity between Ian Smith of Southern Rhodesia and the leaders in Zambia who wouldn't allow us to import our petrol through their borders. There were no roads between Chobe and the rest of Botswana so we were completely dependent on Zambia and were stuck without them allowing us to access petrol.

When our supply was cut off I phoned the Botswana government and they said that they could get my order of petrol through Johannesburg and Francistown then to Rhodesia, travelling via the Victoria Falls where it would clear customs, and finally to us. I didn't want anyone else to know about these involved plans, but while I was discussing the process I heard a dog bark somewhere on the line. This was a private conversation so I said, "Someone is listening to my conversation. Webby, are you there?" A voice came out of the other end of the line and said, "I'm not listening!" That time I had caught him with his pants down! When the petrol tanker eventually arrived I nearly kissed the driver.

We had to deal with all sorts of people – rich and poor, from Eastern European spies and local policemen to tramps and royalty, fisherman and businesspeople – a real mixed bag. We were like a big family, but some were rather peculiar. There was a bachelor, a forester, who would sit at home by himself at a candle-lit dinner wearing a suit. Perhaps he would reminisce about better times back home in England. Major Lamb was also very British. He had a rosy face from all the pink gins – morning, noon and night. This was an easy life for civil servants. There was also a young agricultural guy who used to go skiing with us. He taught me to play bridge.

There were many fun times while we were at Chobe. Janusz recounts an incident when he was staying there with a couple of his friends, Alan and Lesley, Lolly's brother. "We decided that we would entertain the visitors at the Lodge with a New Year's concert," remembers Janusz, "Alan said he would tell jokes and Lesley felt that he could cut a dash if he were to sing opera. I couldn't sing or dance so I had to think hard about what my forte might be. I felt that I had to make the most of my best asset. I went out into the garden and found a good-sized bee. I let it sting me on an extremely vulnerable part. It swelled to gynormous proportions. That evening I started to do what I thought was a very sensuous strip tease. I really did think that it was particularly sexy. Slowly I removed each garment until I was left with only my underpants – but Ala was a spoilsport. As I was removing the last piece of clothing – my underpants, she switched off the lights and all my pain had been for nothing!"

Janusz ties the knot – again!

In 1970 Janusz married Dawn in Durban. It was a big wedding and they decided to come to Chobe for their honeymoon. This was quite a 'happening' as they brought eight people with them. Neville, Eric, Jerry, David and their partners all came along to make sure that the honeymoon was a success. The lady who accompanied David was actually one of Janusz's ex-girlfriends. Perhaps she came along in case Dawn couldn't make him happy? They all had a fantastic time shooting, fishing and game viewing. Lolly managed to overturn a vehicle while they were in it but fortunately no one was hurt. They went waterskiing and Eric was frightened of swimming so they had a lot of fun scaring him half to death.

"I took them all out one night to see crocodiles," recalls Janusz. "I caught one but it was a little too big. It ended up in the boat so everyone leapt out of the boat into the water to get away from the dangerous creature. It was the funniest thing I had ever seen and, of course, Eric had to decide which scared him the most – the water or the crocodile. The crocodile won!"

They stayed for about ten days. On their way home they went to the Victoria Falls Casino and lost all their money.

Janusz tells of their misfortunes: "We had ten pounds left between the ten of us. We needed to buy petrol which cost about five pounds, and then we stopped for breakfast which was another three pounds. I gave the remaining two pounds to our waitress as a tip. We had nothing after that and were a long way from Johannesburg. We had to sell the spare tyre in order to get money for petrol to reach John Coleman's house where we could get help."

Janusz and Dawn are still together – I think she's a saint.

Chris and Ian
lead the life of Riley

It's easy for me to be nostalgic about Chobe. I think back on those halcyon days with fond memories. Not that I live either for, or in the past, but imagining the loveliness of Chobe's nature epitomises all the miracles and beauty of unspoilt creation and remembering the wonderful times we had always brings about a warm glow. It was a great privilege to live in this part of the world. It was the core of Africa. The beauty of the birds, the cry of the fish eagle each morning, being able to sit on the verandah and watch elephants swimming across the river, to see the crocodiles or hear the hippos grunt at night was almost unbelievable. It was all so natural. There were no rules and regulations. It was very hot, but we could do all sorts of things which compensated for the heat. We could go fishing, swimming, game-viewing, have marvellous picnics or cross the river into Zambia or Rhodesia.

For the boys it was a blissful existence. Chris recounts a typical day for him as a little lad. "I would get up in the morning, take my gun and fishing rods, get on a boat and disappear down the Chobe River for the whole day. We [Ian and I] would catch fish or shoot birds and eat them. If we were unlucky and didn't catch anything, we would go back to the Lodge for lunch. Once, we decided to go out camping. We planned to rough it so we didn't take provisions. On the first day we caught nothing. All we could find was a cobra, so we killed and ate it. It was quite delicious. We were living off the wild." The boys were free to eat whenever they felt like it. Going into the bush and eating whatever they caught was a huge adventure.

Chris fondly remembers their unrestricted way of life: "It was a great life. We were scoundrels and sometimes went into the Game Reserve to tease elephants. They used to charge us. We were also charged by a lioness and had to dive into the river to escape – crocodiles or no crocodiles. We didn't think about dangers in those days. We used to swim in the river every day of our lives. Had I known what I do now about crocodiles I would never have been so foolhardy." Chris laughs at the ignorance and carelessness of youth. "We often went up to Crocodile Island which is opposite the place where a hotel has recently been built. There was a lovely big sandbar that was always full of crocodiles. We rationalised in our little boy minds that we would always see a crocodile on the sandbar and be able to get away to safety in time. Once we found a dog there. Some of the local people used to use dogs to lure the crocodiles so that they could shoot them and get their skins.

Ala's Story

The poor little animal we found was just skin and bone and yelping for help. We released and fed it.

I used to sell the fish I caught to mom at the Lodge so that I could make some money. If she did not want to buy my catch I sold it to the Africans who lived in the compound area. I would put an enormous barbel into a wheelbarrow and wheel it up to their houses and bargain until I was satisfied with the price. Sometimes I was by myself when I went on my adventures. At those times Ian did his own thing."

There was never a dull moment at the Lodge. I remember the boys going crocodile hunting with Uncle Janusz – how exciting that was for them! After each hunt they would come back to the Lodge with hair-raising stories of their escapades on the river. I used to have nightmares about them. Once, a crocodile bit into one of Ian's fingers. The bite was so tight that it stopped the flow of blood to the finger. Janusz wedged a knife into the crocodile's mouth and managed to open it slightly so that the finger could be pulled out. All this time dealing with a not very happy and really large wild crocodile. When the finger eventually emerged it was purple.

"We were never short of excitement," grins Chris. "One day we were having lunch in the dining room while mom was in the office on the phone when lightening struck a tree outside the lodge. The tree was uprooted and flung onto the diningroom windows. Glass flew across the room and shards embedded themselves in the opposite wall. Mom was talking on the phone which is one of the most dangerous things you can do in an electric storm. She said that she saw fire travelling up the cable and dropped the receiver just in time. We all ran outside to see the damage. The smell of sulphur was quite considerable. Mom, who was understandably in a state of shock, shouted for us to get inside. I think she was concerned that there would be more lightening. The cutlery on the table all turned gold and glowed.

It was a wild, wild life. Unfortunately, our teacher, Anne Hutchinson, had to return to America which meant the end of our blissful existence."

I sent the boys back to Victoria Falls where they were to stay with a friend while they attended school. I went up there to visit them and found them running wild in the rain forest. I decided that this was not doing much for their education and that they would have to go to a good boarding school in Johannesburg. Of course, they didn't agree with me. They had been very unhappy about leaving Chobe and the thought of going to what they called a 'concentration camp' was the last straw. I decided to give them a choice. Either we sold Chobe and went to live somewhere where they could attend school, or they went away to a good boarding school and came back to Chobe for holidays. They ended up at St David's Marist Brothers College in Inanda, Johannesburg.

"They were so damned strict!" wails Chris. "It was worse than a concentration camp. We used to get a hiding for absolutely nothing, every day. One day, when we were playing soccer, it started pouring with rain. We went and took shelter under a roof and a brother came out and gave us all a caning because he had not given permission for us to stop playing. If somebody did something wrong and did not own up then everyone got six of the best."

The contrast to the free lives they had enjoyed at Chobe must have nearly killed the boys, but they gritted their teeth because they had the prospect of still spending their holidays in that beautiful, wild, wonderful part of the world. They really looked forward to their holidays. There were other boys in similar circumstances so they formed good friendships which must have helped them to keep going.

In spite of their discontent, the boys attended the school for four years. We really missed them. Janusz, who was living in Johannesburg at the time, used to take them out for weekends. They would go to the Vaal River and in Chris's words, "Have an absolute ball." Janusz would have a different girl in tow each time, and they would drive out in a little four-wheel drive car and shoot guinea fowl. Hilda, a friend from Chobe, also helped out with weekend outings.

I used to send pocket money to my children and they were really good boys. Once, when they were about to come home for the school holidays, they decided to buy us a present. They conscientiously saved their pocket money. Ian, who loved cooldrinks and chocolates, was told by Chris that if he wanted to buy something for his mom and dad he would have to drink water instead of Coca-Cola. Most of the boys at the school came from wealthy families and when Chris and Ian said that they wanted to buy their parents a gift, they were taken in a chauffeur-driven Rolls-Royce to a jeweller in Rosebank, one of the most expensive shops around at that time. They eventually chose a beautiful carving set in a box, a gift we really appreciated.

Ian remembers how Lolly used to do elephant control – culling elephants that had become a danger to cultivated lands or villages. Because of his experience, the district commissioner often asked Lolly to go out and destroy these rogue elephants. The boys used to go along. They were still quite young but were able to follow the tracks for as much as two days. The bushmen trackers would lead the way, but this was invaluable learning time for two little boys who were to make the bush their lives.

Ian shot his first elephant when he was 12 years old. When the elephant went down there were several other elephants that surrounded it and tried to get it back onto its feet. They tried to lift it up. Lolly told Ian to fire off a shot over the heads of the elephants in order to frighten them off, but they seemed to be unconcerned about the noise. One of the bushmen fetched a short stick and started to hit it against a hollow log. It sounded like someone chopping wood. The elephants took off immediately as if they found the sound repulsive. Ian will never forget that experience especially how knowledgeable those bushmen were. Elephants are highly intelligent animals and very social in their structure. This was a herd of bulls and their reaction to one of the herd being shot was even more amazing because bonds between male elephants are usually not great. The bonds in a female/calf structure are highly developed. The whole scene must have been very special to witness. Ian says he has never had the desire to go out and shoot another elephant especially with later experiences that he had when he was privileged to get really close to these huge animals. He is the kind of man that has never had a thrill out of hunting per se. I have known him to go out for a whole day hunting impala for the pot and coming home empty-handed. Of course he knows that at times it's absolutely necessary for an animal to be killed. When he shot the elephant it was because it had killed a villager and caused a lot of damage including flattening a complete maize field. Local people have a subsistence lifestyle. If they lose a crop it means that there will be no food.

It's necessary to study the history of an elephant before destroying it. Many elephants that turn nasty have been traumatised as babies during culls. Seeing its whole family destroyed in front of it can easily cause it to behave badly. One should also examine the circumstances of the elephant's actions. An elephant showing aggression needs to be monitored in terms of its possible danger to humans. People often tend to make a huge issue the moment a wild animal is involved.

Chobe had the highest concentration of elephants at the time. After we left the population became so huge that they decimated the riverine vegetation with the result that the Chobe bushbuck disappeared.

We became very friendly with Graham and Di Charles and their family. Graham was writing a thesis on the Chobe bushbuck. They lived in the Parks Board Headquarters in the Reserve and we often visited one another. Graham and I share a birthday and we often shared birthday parties. Their son, Brian, later also got his doctorate in conservation. He introduced the 'campfire' initiative in Zimbabwe by which local communities could benefit. If there were wild animals in the area causing problems to the villages and needed to be destroyed, they would use professional hunters and the profit would be ploughed back into the communities. Committees were formed to identify areas of need such as schools and in this way communities were uplifted. It was a highly successful system of conservation at that time and has helped to preserve much of the Zimbabwe population of elephants. Nowadays there is a lot of poaching and the population is in danger of being decimated – all Brian's good work being undone. Not only is the game suffering but trees are being indiscriminately chopped down for firewood and maize planted. One can't blame them because many people are starving but it's very sad to see a fine country with a fantastic track record in conservation being destroyed. Fortunately Botswana is one of relatively few countries in Africa that is stable. Its policies with regards to wildlife are very sound, which is encouraging.

Of his life in Chobe Ian says, "The average person will never experience what I did. There were vast areas that were uninhabited, wild. We were totally isolated and the nearest places, like Livingstone, were still fairly small villages and, at that time, only accessible on bad dirt roads. It was quite a problem to get our main supplies. To travel the approximately 100 kilometres from Kasane to Maun took about three to four days driving at an average speed of eight kilometres per hour. One also had to pass through tsetse fly country which was an added danger."

Professional game hunters from Kenya accompanied by their wives and kids often stayed with us at Chobe for four or five months during the hunting season. The wives all seemed to be beautiful women with gorgeous figures. They did nothing all day except to lie around the pool drinking pink gins. I had to slog all day long running the Lodge. I didn't envy them. I had very little time to spend on latest fashions and beautifying myself. But I didn't regard these things as important. One day Lolly made a remark about how nice these other women looked, so I thought, "You bugger! I'll fix you."

So when I went to Johannesburg to fetch the children, I bought a mini skirt with a slit up the side, high red boots and a cigarette holder. I remember when Princess Marina visited us: her hairdresser wore this little tight, very short skirt. Because we were so isolated we didn't realise that mini-skirts were the height of fashion and thought her outfit was disgusting. We were surprised, thinking surely she should have enough money to buy more material. How times change! And here was I buying an even shorter skirt. One night, when we weren't very busy in the bar, I sat on the stool in my ridiculously short skirt with my knees sexily crossed, cigarette holder in hand. The kids walked into the pub. They took one look and rushed up to Lolly, "Dad, dad! Come and see what mom's doing!" They were shocked, but it didn't seem to make much impression on Lolly.

There was an upstairs room at the Lodge where people could hold private parties. The children's room was right next to this, so when they were there on holiday, they used to listen to the parties all night.

"In the morning, when we awoke," remembers Chris, "we would go into the pub and collect all the *stompies* (cigarette stubs) from the ashtrays and try smoking them and drink anything left in the glasses. Mom caught us. She took us down to the garden, lit a cigarette and said, "smoke!" We coughed and smoked, smoked and coughed and got really sick. It was the last time we ever touched a cigarette. Mom then said that we should not drink from other people's leftovers. She poured drinks from a bottle that looked lethal. She made us drink this vile stuff which caused us to be even more sick. It did, however, cure us for life."

My mother, who ran the off-sales and did the flowers, had a friend, a little lady,

Mrs Stapa. We called her Aunt Lila. She was delightful, always happy and full of fun. She had a farm near Livingstone and after her husband died she refused to give up the land, but had to continue in her job as the manageress of the shoe store, Bata. One day as Lolly was driving to Livingstone, he encountered a broken-down vehicle. As far as he could see it had been abandoned. He went to investigate and there he saw this little lady underneath the car trying to fix it. This was the start of our friendship with her. She also loved animals. Some time after she had moved to Chobe to help my mother, an African man brought in a little otter. She asked if she could buy it and the animal grew up in her room. His name was Maciek which is Polish for Matthew. He was a real character. At breakfast we would find him waiting for the visitors to order their bacon and eggs. He loved bacon and would jump onto the table and steal it. He also loved butter. In spite of his stealing ways, the guests loved him. On one occasion Maciek and his friend, our fox terrier, stole the ice from the drinks of our guests and got a little tight. Maciek proceeded to do his gymnastic tricks which amused and enchanted the onlookers. He loved Aunty Lila. When she was away for her breaks he missed her and was impossible. He used to mess in the Lodge and one day he got into a suitcase belonging to two old ladies and tore quite a few garments. On another occasion, at the time of sanctions against Rhodesia, a Rhodesian client came and put up his precious tent he had recently imported from Germany – precious because such things were unobtainable in any of the shops in Rhodesia. Maciek tore the thing to shreds. When Aunty Lila returned that animal talked to her. He carried on with noises, crying and talking, "How could you leave me?" and his behaviour changed completely. He would listen to her and not mess inside. He behaved beautifully and was a joy to have.

Maciek loved to go into the river and challenge other male otters. One day he returned with part of his claw missing. It had probably been bitten off in a skirmish. Claw or no claw we all loved him.

A film crew from the United States booked in for two weeks. I could see how fascinated they were with Maciek. After their first day they appeared nervous and edgy and said that they'd received an urgent message and would have to leave. Our communications systems were not very modern and it would have been impossible for them to have received any messages in that time so it was a little strange. But they left and Maciek disappeared. It seemed certain that the film crew had stolen him. Years later when we were living in Nelspruit, we saw a film about the escapades of an otter. Suddenly I shouted, "That's Maciek. Look, he has a missing claw!" It was really sad.

One day a man arrived with a bird. We thought it was a baby fish eagle. Aunty Lila felt sorry for it because it was probably destined for the pot and so she bought it for fifteen shillings. It turned out to be a vulture. He used to sit above the Lodge and people would ask, "What is that vulture waiting for?"

We had one guest, an elderly man, who loved to go for walks. The vulture seemed to wait for him and then follow. The gentleman did not like it very much because it looked as if the bird was waiting for him to die.

Many years after we all left Chobe, Sonja (who was Chris's wife at that time), Lolly, Chris and I went to visit Aunty Lila. She was living in Harare (the capital of Zimbabwe). She was so thrilled to see us. She has since passed away. So many memories!

Not far from the Lodge, on an island, was the South African police post. They often visited us for drinks. One day they came with a little baboon. It was an orphan so we took it and kept it at the Lodge. Eventually we released it into the bush. We loved the animals, but always wanted them to return to the wild if it was possible.

The police used to get drunk on their visits to us. Once when crossing the river on a return trip one of them was killed by an elephant. The animals around us were wild. It was a good idea to remember this and unwise to take chances with them.

Mrs Fitzpatrick of 'Jock of the Bushveld' fame used to visit us. She and Lolly used to camp out in tents at Serrandellas. They slept on two beds under the trees and hung mosquito netting over the beds for protection. Mrs Fitzpatrick loved Lolly because he took her on really wild trips. One day Mrs Fitzpatrick arrived in a truck. She and her party had been on safari. On their return journey to Maun the truck broke down and they were stuck for days. Lolly eventually received a message from them with a plea for help. They suggested in the message that he bring plenty of spare parts for the truck with him. Lolly was a real junk collector. He said that you never knew when something would come in handy. He collected any junk he could lay his hands on. This time his collection came in handy and he was able to help Mrs Fitzpatrick and her group.

Because of the war, apartheid, and many other political factors, there was turmoil in Botswana. There was a lot of anti-white feeling and we felt unsafe. All the refugees fleeing South Africa and heading for Zambia went through Chobe and were not too pleased to encounter white people running the only lodge. There was an Arab man who was waiting to get into Zambia. For some reason or other, probably because we were white, he refused to pay his bill. I argued with him for some time but he continued to be difficult. Eventually I phoned the police who came and fetched him and took him to the police station. Once he got there he changed his tune and said he would pay. On his return to the lodge he once again refused so was rearrested and put into jail.

Staying on at the lodge became untenable in terms of the antagonism towards us. Although the people in Botswana were never really a problem – the main problem came from outsiders – we were in real danger. We had to accept the situation. Active terrorists in Caprivi curtailed our freedom. Ken Momson was badly injured

Ala's Story

in an attack while taking equipment up to Katimo in his barge. We had to be very cautious about where we went and started to feel restricted. The only way to get the boys safely to school was to fly them there. We accepted the need for change.

Eventually we decided to leave Chobe, mostly because we missed the children. There was a man and his wife who frequently visited us. He never went on game drives or did much at Chobe but he seemed to have his eye on the Lodge. He would stand and watch me working in the office. One day he asked if we would consider selling. I said, "Never!"

But we had to move on to somewhere else so that we could all be safe and together. Lolly had bought a farm, Buffelshoek, next to the Kruger National Park. Lolly and the two boys used to go down there and build dams. In fact, there's still a dam that's named after him, one that he'd built with our sons. The boys enjoyed these trips.There were vast herds of wildebees and zebra in the area. Animals roamed freely and there were no fences. There were few people there at the time. I didn't like the arrangement because I felt it was a waste of money. We didn't need a nature reserve in South Africa. We were already living in the best place on earth. I insisted Lolly sell it. He tried to sell it to his brother, Clyde, who had bought a development in Hazyview that had ten shops. Hazyview is a small town in what was then the Eastern Transvaal and is now Mpumalanga. Clyde said if Lolly would take over his Hazyview investment he would swap it for the Buffelshoek place. I felt the shops would be more profitable because they were part of a business and that was something that I understood.

Meanwhile, another friend, Derek Verster, convinced us to buy a share in a five-bedroomed house at San Martino in Mozambique. We picked up the kids in Johannesburg and flew in our twin engine plane to see the house. It was lovely and really inexpensive so we bought it and we shared many happy hours there over the years, with Derek and many other friends.

When we decided to sell Chobe, Lolly flew to Johannesburg to see the chap who had been interested in buying our Lodge. He wasn't buying for himself but on behalf of Percival Tours. They flew back to Chobe together. Stock was immediately taken and the new owners took over.

After we left, Kasane closed down completely. The manager was later deported. We felt the reasons for their deportation were trumped up, but a definite sign of the times.

After the deal went through we went on a cruise to Mauritius with Janusz, Dawn, her mother and sister and Lolly's brother. There were 13 of us all together. We were really sad to leave Chobe. We left Mother and Aunty Lila in a house in Kazangula for six months. The cruise was lovely and for the first 24 hours no one slept. We were too busy eating wonderful food and losing our money in casinos.

Then we moved to South Africa and stayed in Hazyview for a while. We owed a lot of money on the Hazyview property and had a huge overdraft. For once the bank looked after us. Because we owed them so much money we were precious to them. They took us to banquets and generally feted us. We tried to establish a township development in Hazyview but it wasn't really our scene, mostly because it involved greasing palms which was not our way of doing business. We then went to live in Nelspruit where we stayed with Clyde in his magnificent double-storey house. I felt that I would love to own a house like that. So we took over the bond and paid cash for the rest and I was very happy there although I never really got over my sadness of leaving Chobe.

It was so wonderful being with the children in Nelspruit.

Lolly wanted to bring all his collection of junk with him when we moved from Chobe. He had to make several trips back to get all our stuff, so every time he went away I managed to throw some of his rubbish away, but a lot of it ended up in Nelspruit. When we bought the house it came complete with a lot of lovely antiques. I felt we really didn't need all Lolly's junk in such a beautiful place.

I was delighted to once again be in civilisation. It was a pleasure to be able to go to a hairdresser when I wanted to, to get books from a public library and to attend yoga classes. In the beginning I was very lonely because I didn't know anyone. When a neighbour from over the road visited us she was formally dressed, in a hat and gloves. She probably thought we were really posh people because of our grand house. She was Afrikaans-speaking and didn't understand English. It was difficult to communicate. She was the only neighbour who made any effort. I used to take the children to the park where I would sit on my own and watch them feeling rather conspicuous and lonely.

Our beautiful house in Nelspruit

Ala's Story

Things changed when we joined a church community. We met lots of people who became our friends and my social life started to pick up. We had parties and went out often.

Lolly suffered a minor nervous breakdown after leaving Chobe. The move must have been traumatic for him. As a result of this he lost his eyesight for a while. We were at Savuti with the children at the time. Obviously we were very worried about it. A specialist diagnosed the breakdown and said that it was the cause of the blindness. As a result, I felt he was becoming too dependent on me so when John Coleman offered him a job culling animals I felt that it would be better for Lolly to go without me. Lolly, however, refused to go on his own. We spent two weeks living in tents on the banks of the Limpopo River and, while the men were out, I sat in the river trying to keep cool. We were not really equipped to entertain so when some of our friends unexpectedly turned up for a visit I was desperate because I didn't have enough food to cook them breakfast. I said to Lolly, "Go out and see if you can find us an ostrich egg."

He was successful and I was able to feed twenty people with one egg, served with biltong and bread.

On our return trip we had a car accident. I had a smart Plymouth convertible at the time. Like Janusz, I love nice things, but unlike him I do not live beyond my means. If I want something and I can afford it, I buy it. The accident happened when we were driving the children back to school from the Limpopo River and Lolly was driving quite fast. It was late at night and we didn't see a kudu that jumped right in front of the car. The radiator was completely smashed, but fortunately we weren't hurt. We managed to get a lift to a nearby farm and Lolly was able to patch up the car so that we could get back to Johannesburg. I was sad about my car. We spent that night at a motel and took the children to school the next day.

Back home Lolly started to really get on my nerves. He seemed to have nothing to do and when he started telling me how I should cut up the onions I knew the time had come to get him out of the house. Wally Durr, a friend of ours, was running a travel agency and a safari company that took people on trips to the Kruger National Park. He asked Lolly if he would do some driving for the company. I was delighted. At last Lolly would be out of my hair while doing something he enjoyed. Men are never at their best when they suffer from boredom.

Nelspruit was good for me. I started a book club and became involved with the boys' school as well as their scout group. The principal of the school asked me to organise and run a sports day at which I would have to cater for about 6 000 people. Of course I didn't do it all by myself and had a lot of help from other parents. It was fabulous and I had many compliments. I did a lot of voluntary work in the town and also opened a tuck shop for Lowveld High School when Ian began secondary school. Mr Gray, the principal, always said how grateful he was for the

Lolly and I

money we raised. I tried to run the tuck shop and serve only healthy foods. We got fresh fruit from the local farmers; we emphasised a healthy diet. After I left they unfortunately went back to serving junk food.

I suppose I was really too involved. I was also vice-chairlady of Child Welfare. It was run by an elderly lady by the name of Mrs Greathead. She seemed to be more than 100 years old, annoyed everyone and always wanted to have her say. She was a wealthy woman who owned big farms in the area. She once decided to introduce Coca-Cola into the area. She negotiated a deal with a guy who was importing Coke. When he arrived with cases of the fizzy drink, she asked him where his political affiliation lay. When he said that he belonged to the National Party, and not to the United Party, she sent him and his cases packing. When she came into a meeting we would wink at each other and then sit patiently, listen to her and agree with what she had to say. If anyone disagreed there would be trouble.

Wally Durr was offered a good job with the South African tourism board in Switzerland. He decided to sell his tourist business in Nelspruit and we bought the safari side of it – that is, the part that was involved with taking people on tours. Friends of ours, Ernest and Darlene, bought the agency part of the business. I didn't want to get too involved, but I needed to help Lolly to get going. I continued to do my own thing during the mornings and went into the business at lunchtime; it brought in a good income. It paid the school fees, and although there were sanctions against South Africa at the time and the tourist trade suffered as a result, we managed well. We kept the income from the sale of Chobe in the bank as our security.

I was still quite young at this stage, just over 40. Someone told me I shouldn't be happy because 40 was a terrible age. All ones pains and aches would begin. I waited for this to happen and it never did. When I turned 50 I thought, "Well, now it will start!" But it never happened. Nor did the pains begin at 60. I have appreciated every day and enjoyed my life to the full. Even now at 70-plus I relish every day. To be honest I did begin to feel a few little niggles after I turned 70.

Mother stayed with us and she helped to keep the house and the garden beautiful. At the age of 70 she started yoga classes. She helped in so many ways especially with the Red Cross in Nelspruit because she remembered how they had helped us when we were in Siberia.

True to form, Chris kept snakes in his room and a python in an enclosure. Of course the python had to be fed but, fortunately, they hibernate in winter. He bought rabbits to feed the snakes but my mother could not bear the thought of those rabbits being snake food. She used to plead with Lolly, "Lolly, please do something or the python will kill those rabbits. I can't bear the thought of that."

Lolly snapped back, "Keep your nose out of it. It has nothing to do with you!"

The python, however, grew so used to the rabbits that they would sit together without the rabbits coming to any harm. I think that my mother must have prayed that the rabbits would be safe! Chris then bought a guinea pig but it was a female and had babies so we felt we couldn't feed it to the python because the babies needed to be looked after by their mother.

Inevitably the boys grew up and left home. Ian went to Agricultural School for a bit and then on to the army for two years. The army was a place where there was bullying and fearful induction practices. Those first few months were not very pleasant for Ian. He once phoned in an awful state, so Lolly and I went and stayed in a caravan at Sodwana Bay, near where he was stationed, in order to have a weekend with him to try to boost his morale. After the first bit Ian settled down. Chris went to Pietermaritzburg University and then also on to the army where he became a lieutenant. After his two year army stint he went to Pretoria to study nature conservation. Although the army days were something that had to be lived through, I have no regrets and being there probably toughened them up a bit. The freedom they had experienced in Chobe was not good preparation for the regimented life in the army.

I suffered the 'empty nest' syndrome when the boys left. One day I had a houseful of men and the next the house seemed deserted. My solution was to throw myself into social life and charity work.

The ten years we spent in Nelspruit were filled with fun and playtime. I loved it there. We had so many friends. Life was great! But, with my life, I should have known that things would not stay static for long.

Part 4
Tshukudu
1980 ~ present

The beginning of the end

Lolly, being a bush man and having experienced such an unsettled life, was not satisfied with living in the town. Visiting friends and going to parties didn't bring him much joy so he started driving around the countryside with his two friends, Julio Ramponi and Willy Doyer, looking for something that he could buy in order to create a reserve for animals. For so many years he had been a hunter and felt he needed to return something to nature. He wanted to settle among animals, where he could find peace and tranquility. At the time I didn't take his wanderings very seriously. I thought it was a fleeting whim that he would get over. I was the one, however, who was to be disillusioned.

Lolly's ramblings took him to Vaalwater, a desolate place in what is now the North West Province. On his return to Nelspruit his excitement was ill-concealed. He said he'd found a farm there and thought it might be the ideal place for his animal project. Our friend, Derek, was staying with us in Nelspruit at the time. He took me aside and joked, "You know, you will never play bridge in Vaalwater – they have probably never heard of it, and the guys still wear braces to keep up their pants. It would be like the end of the world for you. Think twice before you commit yourself to moving to this unlikely part of the world."

Of course, this was many years ago, and I'm sure that things in Vaalwater are very different now!

Derek had a serious talk to Lolly and eventually we were able to dissuade him from buying the farm. Lolly, however, was not to be deterred. He was determined to find his dream place. His travels took him into the Northern Province (now Limpopo). He drove all around areas he felt might interest him. This included a place called Hoedspruit

One day Lolly returned from one of his trips with the news that he had found his sanctuary. "It's the most wonderful place in all the world," he said. "Nobody has lived there for years. It used to belong to President Diederichs. After his death the property was repossessed by the banks. The place is just too wonderful and has so many prospects." My heart stopped beating. I knew what was to come.

"I'll take you there and show you what its like," promised Lolly.

So we made our first journey together to what was to become Tshukudu. At that time it consisted of three farms – Vienna, Paris and Berlin. The farms had been named after cities of Europe because the surveyors were originally from there and probably thought the names would bring some sort of culture to this desolate land. There were other farms with similar names in the area.

My first impression of the place was not very hopeful. Everything was brown. There were no green trees or lush wild flowers – only thickets of gnarled scrub trees and scattered patches of thorn bush. Dust from the worn dirt roads swirled in dense brown clouds. An inhospitable landscape of flat, never-ending desolation as far as the eye could see. As we drove towards the house the splendour of the mountains was behind us so there was nothing to relieve the wretchedness of the scene. Eventually we arrived at what had been described as the house. It was nothing more than a run-down, deserted *pondokie* (humble, broken-down dwelling). The place was falling apart and I saw evidence of rats, bats and things that were too awful to contemplate. I had seen enough. I got back into the car, burst into tears and said, "This is not for me. I'm never going to live here."

Of course, I should have known that with three against one it's impossible to win. Ian and Chris were very supportive of their father. I was outnumbered. Both my boys were excited about the place. Both had aspirations to be bush men just like their father, and here was the ideal place for them to fulfil their dreams. At this stage Ian was out of the army and working at a lodge in the Timbavati private game reserve, owned by friends of ours.

Of this rather radical move Ian says, "Dad still wanted to get back into the bush. He was also very conscious of the demise of wildlife in Africa and wanted to do something to help by having his own little reserve. I think that when he saw this place and managed to acquire the land his dream became a reality. Mom didn't need another upheaval. She was happy in Nelspruit. She had a lot of friends there and was totally involved. She had everything a lady could wish for on her doorstep. But she was always up for a challenge."

Lolly visited the banks that held the debt on the farms and made an offer. He was determined that he was going to go through with his ambitious dream. His was not the only bid for the farms. There were about six other interested parties. When I heard this I felt safe because it seemed unlikely that our bid would win. Luck wasn't on my side and Lolly was awarded the farms. The news was announced on my birthday – 6 June 1980.

Ian's employer from Timbavati flew Ian into Nelspruit for my birthday. For Ian it was Christmas and a birthday rolled into one. He left his job and moved into the 'house' on the farm. Shortly after that Lolly followed. Ian lived in the rondawel at the back of the old house. There wasn't electricity or other creature comforts, but for him it was a fantastic time, although difficult, because he was forced to do his own cooking and laundry as well as all the other chores necessary to build up the farm.

Now we had to raise the funds to pay the banks. We had a certain amount of money from selling the lodge at Chobe, but that was far from enough. So our beautiful double-storey house with its lovely gardens had to be put onto the market. I had to say goodbye to my dream home, the place I thought I would live in for the rest of my life. We bought the house for R50 000 sold it for R75 000 and today it is on the market for more than a million. Our business, too, had to be sold, and all our pension money and savings were added to the pot. Even so we still did not have enough to cover the huge debt. Lolly seemed blissfully unaware of my trauma, and was happy to simply move out and go to stay on the derelict farm.

We sold our business, Bushveld Safaris, to the company with which we had been sharing premises, Magnum Airlines, and they asked me to stay on for six months, an arrangement which pleased me! I hated the thought of moving to the farm. There was nothing there to entice me to the place. It was not in any state to generate an income so we needed any money that I could earn. I saw the farm project as the biggest gamble we had ever undertaken.

The property was more than 6 000 hectares and it all had to be maintained. Roads had to be built, pumps fixed, fire-breaks cleared and many other things had to be done. It was a huge job and, after selling off the piece of land on the other side of the railway line, fences needed to be put up. And more buildings had to be constructed. For the first year they only worked on the essentials. Much later, Ian also had to start taking the tourists around. Only after eight years did we employ other rangers. In those days people did not necessarily want to see the 'big five', but seemed to be more interested in the whole bush experience.

Originally our farm extended beyond the railway line at the back, but partly because it was difficult to control poaching because of its isolated nature, and partly because we desperately needed the money to repay our banks, we decided to sell off this piece of land. The group to which we sold ran a game capturing company. The owners were a veterinarian called Blackie Swart and an ex-game warden from the Kruger National Park, Thuys Maritz. They established all their capture bomas on the property. Les Carlisle, who worked for Blackie, became good friends with Chris and Ian. Ian had known Les from the time he had spent at Timbavati Private Game Reserve, on the western border of the Kruger National Park, as well as from school days in Nelspruit. Les had worked in a different part of Timbavati to Ian but they had enjoyed many parties together.

Ian enjoys telling me stories of his time at Timbavati. With the help of Mike Heramb he managed his camp at Timbavati with about 35 beds while Les worked at Motswari under another manager. One day Ian and Mike decided to have a combined birthday party. Everyone came to the camp and they were well into the celebration when they heard lions roaring fairly close by. They decided to see if they could find them. As Mike ran around a corner to get the Land Rover, he tripped over an hyena that had its head in the dustbin. The two went for quite a tumble and there was a bit of moaning, mostly from Mike. He eventually got to the Land Rover and the whole crowd climbed in. They drove around the area but couldn't find any trace of lions. When they got back they found the lions had taken up residence on a slab of cement that was in the garage at the back of the property. One chap decided he would offer the lions a can of beer. Needless to say when he approached, the lions they charged him and he had to be rescued with the vehicle. They went back to the boma and had a good party. The lions eventually went off and headed north.

At about 2am the chaps from Motswari thought it was time to go home because they had to work the next day. Les and another friend had come to the party on scramblers; one could hear the off-road motorbikes as they disappeared into the bush. As they rounded a corner they came across four lionesses with their cubs coming towards them. They didn't think it advisable to try to ride through the group as lionesses are very aggressive, especially when they have cubs. They turned their bikes planning to make a hasty retreat only to find their way barred by a huge male lion. The safest alternative seemed to chance their luck through the lionesses. They revved their bikes and took off. Fortunately they made it.

The rest of the group, behind the two on scramblers, was in a small pick up truck. A tall fellow by the name of George had passed out and was put in the back of the pick up but, because of his height, his feet hung over the tailgate. Three others were squashed in front. They, too, rounded a corner and found themselves in the midst of a pride of lions. The big male walked past, brushed against the driving mirror and saw the chap in the back. George woke up and looked straight into the eyes of the lion. He knew he was drunk, but also realised that he was not dreaming. He pounded on the window between him and those in the cab and yelled, "Hey, you guys! There are lions out here!" The boys in the front were laughing so much that they stalled the pick up. All George could do was to pull his feet up and pray. They got home safely but the experience had sobered George up completely.

One day, Ian, Andy and Rooker were on their way home with an American lady. They saw a big python in the road so they stopped the vehicle and jumped out to catch it. They decided to take the snake back with them. Andy was driving and Rooker was holding onto the snake. After a while he felt that the snake was too still and was worried that he had been holding it too tightly and had suffocated it. He held it up to his cheek to check to see if it was still alive and it bit him. He jumped out of the car with blood running down his face, crying out, "This is a dangerous snake. I'm going to die!" With that he proceeded to roll about on the ground. The lady was really frightened. She jumped off the vehicle and ran down the road to the camp and woke Pat Donaldson who was the manager. Pat was furious. His first reaction was to fire all the reprobates, but finally he saw the funny side of things. A python's bite is harmless – it's a constrictor.

These bush experiences were crucial to Ian's development as a bush man. He had a good time with some fantastic people and was always in for a bit of fun, but learnt caution and being able to judge just how far one can go with a wild animal.

The business venture of the group to whom we had originally sold the piece of land across the railway line unfortunately came to nothing and the bank eventually repossessed the property. It was then bought by Peter Milstein who has been responsible for some wonderful bird books. He later sold the land which was sub-divided into plots for a wildlife estate.

Setting up Tshukudu

The trio of farms were situated about four kilometres outside Hoedspruit. The little town itself was nothing. There was a café on the railway station and a little centre with a small Post Office in the middle of town. Once, when I had driven Chris and his school swimming team from Nelspruit to attend a gala in Phalaborwa, we had passed through Hoedspruit. The children asked for something to drink as it was a particularly hot day, so I looked for a place to buy something. We found the station café and managed to buy cool drinks. I remember thinking to myself, "Who would want to live in this God-forsaken place?"

There was absolutely nothing there. It looked foul. Little did I know that one day I would have to call it home!

Once the house in Nelspruit had been sold we had to transfer all our furniture to the farm. Needless to say I had to go there with the boys to clean the place up to make it livable, while Lolly decided to go fishing.

The boys also decided they wanted to move there. For them this was heaven; for me it was hell. In order to relocate we borrowed a little truck and moved our household room by room. Our home in Nelspruit was very big and we had a lot of stuff – far too much for the ramshackle house on the farm. I really don't know how I survived this time. It was heartbreaking leaving my home, and the prospect of living in this wasteland held no joy for me. Anyway, for the time being, I was

Lolly, a few years later, still enjoying his favourite pastime – fishing

to stay on in Nelspruit. The plan was that I would stay there from Monday to Thursday and then spend the weekends on the farm, helping to make it a viable proposition. Fortunately, John Bescoby at Magnum Airlines agreed that I could promote the farm as part of my other work. The only concept I could promote was for groups to have lunch there. The groups would be on a Bushveld Safaris tour from Nelspruit, driving through the Kruger National Park and then on to Blyde River Canyon. I could re-route the tour so that they would have lunch at the farm. This meant I needed to travel there for the day in order to provide the food. Friends were enormously supportive. They would go with me, don their aprons and help with the cooking and serving and then travel back to Nelspruit with me. People seemed to love it here. They saw it as an unspoiled piece of Africa. I saw it as an abomination. It was isolated bush with telephones that had to be cranked up. Anyway, that was how it all started.

For Chris the farm was an instant love affair. From the beginning he spent as much time there as he could, leaving the army base in Pretoria at every opportunity. He moved there permanently around three years after we bought it. At first he slept in the garage which doubled as an old tool room.

There was one little *rondawel* on the farm which we tried to let out. The first people who came to spend a night were a couple who came to the Nelspruit office trying to book accommodation in the Kruger Park for a weekend. It was a long weekend and the Park camps were completely full. I phoned around to places close to the reserve but without any luck. As a last resort I said to them, "How would you like to stay at a little private place that has recently opened up? There is only one rondawel and not much game, but it would give you the opportunity to sit around a bush fire and enjoy nature at its best." I didn't tell them it was my place or the fact that I hated it there!

The man worked for an oil company in Maputo, Mozambique. His wife was Yvonne. Amazingly, I made the sale and they arrived on the farm. When they checked in they saw the name 'Sussens'. Bells went off and the husband asked his wife where they had seen that name before. Yvonne replied, "I'm sure that was the name of the lady who sold us this deal." Lo and behold, who should appear to cook their food but Mrs Sussens! We became close friends and they visited us many times. Unfortunately, the husband passed away and Yvonne returned to her native country, Norway.

The original house is the one that we still use as the lodge. But in the early days it had three bedrooms, a small dining room and a tiny kitchen. There wasn't a lounge. We eventually turned the bedrooms into the lounge. On weekends, when we didn't have guests, I helped patch up the old house. This was often hard manual labour.

The original *rondawel* still stands. We seldom use it because it has no view, but it does come in useful when we need to accommodate a family.

The whole place is steeped in history. President Diederichs was said to lie on a bed outside the rondawel gazing up at the stars. He probably dreamt of a great future for the area once the air force base had been installed at Hoedspruit.

We could accommodate four people in the rondawel, but we sometimes only had one guest. But, however many there were, we would sit in the boma in the evenings and entertain them with stories because there was so little game to see – only the animals that wandered in from neighbouring reserves because there wasn't proper fencing.

Friends asked me if there was some way in which they could help me. Tina and Rita helped a lot with the catering. This also meant I had company travelling back and forth to the farm. It was lonely driving through the trust and I felt perfectly safe on my own but it was always good to have company.

Magnum Airlines approached me and asked if I couldn't perhaps work for them for a bit longer. We were still struggling financially and the higher salary was a major attraction, so I agreed. My week usually began at 4am on Mondays when I left the farm for Nelspruit. It was a drive of 175 kilometers and took two and a half hours. I stayed in a room close to a swimming pool that was part of a friend's home. Connie van Wyk offered me this accommodation, and, although it was very comfortable, I wasn't happy. I had lost my home, I hated the farm, I was separated from my family, my heart was broken. It was difficult to keep my head above water.

The time was right to open a game lodge. We had big dreams. We realised that the best way to make a go of it was to interest overseas as well as local tourists.

We didn't have the money to build more accommodation, but our old friend, Pat French, whom we had known before we were married, asked if he could put up a rondawel where he could stay when he visited us. This meant that we could now offer six beds, and the potential to make a little money was there. Another cottage was paid for by Seun Beneke who we think of as one of the family and he visits us two or three times a year. Years later the last cottage was funded by Ed Bailey from America. He is a paraplegic and had visited all the lodges in the area, in Botswana and the Caprivi Strip. He and his wife, Gloria, love Africa. One day someone recommended us. We had no facilities for wheelchairs and they only stayed a few days. They loved it here and the next time they stayed for a week and then another time for two weeks and then for a month. They wanted better facilities so they asked us to put up a cottage that was wheelchair friendly and were prepared to pay for it. They have been coming for years and years and have many friends among our other regular guests. Once Ed and Gloria, stayed for seven months. Last time Gloria came with Pat Tweedie (a regular Tshukudu visitor). Unfortunately, Ed had a nasty accident while driving his handicapped-friendly converted car. He was injured and has been unable to visit recently. He still hopes to return one day.

Fortune favoured us and Bushveld Safaris decided to include us in its game reserve package. Visitors would spend one night at the Kruger National Park, one night with us, then on to the Blyde River Canyon and a night at Cybele before returning to Nelspruit. Many people who came on these tours returned to us and became our close friends.

There were very few animals on the farm when we took it over. President Diederichs, although not a bad guy, had a son who loved shooting at everything that moved. There was even evidence of trees being shot at. When we first came here we found a storeroom full of butcher's hooks and heaps of hunting gear. The only animals left on the farm were a few giraffe and a couple of wildebeest and impala. We later found a big pack of about 30 wild dogs, including puppies, and that was fun. Animals, including lions, also wandered in and out from the Kruger Park and other neighbouring private game farms.

Even after six months the farm was not making money. Ian fixed up some of the roads and my mother came and helped out for a while, but without funds we couldn't do anything radical. The one thing that we did build was a swimming pool. The whole property is on rocks. There is only a thin layer of soil covering them. So about two or three years after the Tshukudu adventure started Chris decided to build a swimming pool. The boys attempted to dig a hole but discovered that it was solid rock. While in the military Chris was with the army's engineering division so, of course, had learned about explosives and blowing things up. He made an explosive device to blow a hole for the proposed pool. He put a huge charge in and positioned tyres all around to stop rocks flying and causing damage. The explosion was so violent that there were rocks everywhere. The tyres had not been much help and they all landed on the garage roof along with a lot of other debris. The explosion had made quite a big hole, but not big enough so they had to build up the sides in order to get the depth that was wanted. We wanted a very deep pool because the temperature gets so high in summer that depth is needed to keep the water as cool as possible.

Janusz's parting gift

Before leaving South Africa for Australia, where he planned to settle, Janusz gave me a couple of things. One was a double-sized waterbed.

At about that time Lolly exported some animals, including elephants from other farms, to a Taiwan zoo. On his return he told me about some people he had met in Taiwan and that he really wanted to bring them to visit South Africa to see the animals in their natural habitat. I thought we could expect about two people which was fine as at that time we had two rondawels and the cottage, but Lolly told me he expected a party of around 14 people. There was no way that I could accommodate so many people at one time so I hired a bushveld safari vehicle and booked seven of the guests to go to the Kruger Park while the other seven stayed with us and planned that the two groups would swop after a few days. On their exchange day they all met at Tshukudu for lunch. The lunch was a great success, but I was somewhat nonplussed when one of them came to me and said that they didn't want to go to the Kruger Park, but all wanted to stay at Tshukudu. I said that it wouldn't be possible. I didn't have enough accommodation and had already booked for them to visit the Park.

"No, no," he said, "We will sleep on the floor."

Lolly came to me and said, "There is no way that they will go to the Park. Whatever you say they are still staying. They are adamant!"

I racked my brains. Six of them could sleep in the cottage because I could put a double bed on the verandah. Four could sleep on the waterbed that Janusz had bequeathed – after all, they were small in stature and it was a big waterbed. Although I had to smile at the image of four Taiwanese gentlemen rocking and rolling all night on the waterbed. So all of them stayed and had a very good time.

After the Taiwanese group's visit Chris claimed the waterbed. It later fell apart, but fortunately not while our Taiwanese visitors were sleeping on it!

People who visited the lodge returned many times. One such person was Pat Tweedie who came back twice a year for 30 years. She once told me a story about one of her stays here. One morning she awoke and was puzzled by the fact that, although the curtains at the window were drawn, there was little light coming in. Light was streaming in from the front of the room, so she found this phenomenon difficult to understand. She arose from bed to make a closer inspection and found that a huge elephant, probably Tembo, was feeding on the flowers directly outside the window thus blocking out most of the sunlight. Pat died in 2004, but this book gets its name from her story and her memory will always be alive. We have also remembered her in the last video we made of Tshukudu.

I think that my love affair with the place started once Tshukudu began to show some income. It took many years before I didn't have to worry about the finances. The first ten years were the hardest, although we did have a lot of fun. There was a rowdy crowd in the area, so at times it was worse than the 'Wild West'! We even had shoot-outs in the pub – like at Ian's bachelor's party – although, fortunately, guests weren't shooting at each other, but at the buffalo heads on the walls!

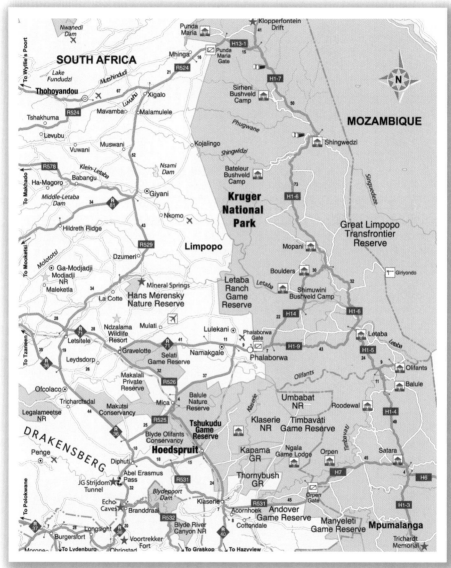

Lic. No. 51107brand - © MapStudio 2007, www.mapstudio.co.za

Tshukudu Game Reserve's location – adjacent to the Kruger – is brilliant

Ala's Story

Jerry the giraffe

Ian recalls how Jerry came to Tshukudu: "At that time they were doing capture on giraffe. They would dart them and then sell them to generate a little much-needed income. There were a lot of giraffe on the farm. They would put the sedated giraffe into a special truck and take them to their new homes. While busy tracking giraffe they came across a kill. Lions had killed a giraffe and were feeding on it. A little bit away was a new-born baby. It could hardly walk. The lions had taken advantage of the weakened state of the mother giraffe. Ian captured the baby and took it back to Tshukudu. And so Jerry came into our lives."

Of course he had to be fed! Ian took on the task of looking after him. He used a two litre Coca-Cola bottle with a teat, and Jerry had to be fed every two hours, day and night. So began Ian's introduction to 'motherhood'. I remember seeing Ian with that sleep deprived look of a new mother who has to feed her baby at all times of the night. Black rings under his eyes and walking around like a zombie. Of course he still had to do his normal daily tasks.

Giraffe are difficult to hand rear. One weekend when I was at Tshukudu I saw how awful Ian looked. I said, "You go and have a good night's sleep and I'll look after Jerry."

After struggling to get him to feed from the bottle, I began to think that this was not practical. I filled the basin with milk and he immediately started to drink. This made life so much easier. So from then on Ian fed him from the basin.

Jerry was the first of our 'orphans' at Tshukudu. There were many more to follow. Everybody loved Jerry. He seemed to enjoy being with humans. Giraffe are always popular with game lovers and to have a giraffe standing in the middle of the road to welcome guests was a big hit. Cars would have to stop because he refused to move out of the way. He would then walk up to the car, put his head in the window and sniff every person in it. If he heard schoolchildren arriving he would always go to meet them.

Once, one of our neighbours came across and he had a labourer sitting in the back of a little Suzuki jeep. It had a canvas roof stretched over a frame. Jerry put his head underneath the canopy to sniff the labourer, who hurriedly moved to the other side of the vehicle. Jerry walked around the car and put his head in on the other side. Once again the labourer shot across the seat. As Jerry moved to pull his head out of the canopy he hooked his horns in the top of the frame and in trying to straighten his neck he physically lifted the jeep off the ground. The chap thought Jerry was about to throw the vehicle over so he dived out screaming like a madman. The poor giraffe was so surprised. All he'd wanted to do was to greet the man and here he was making all that fuss.

Sylvia with Jerry

When I was at Tshukudu I liked to invite friends to play bridge. My bridge friends loved Jerry. He was really the most beloved animal and would never intentionally hurt anyone, but if someone ran away from him he thought it was a game and would give chase. June Coppen, one of my bridge friends, was confronted by Jerry who went to smell her. She got a fright and ran behind a bush. Of course Jerry went off in pursuit and round the bush they went. June was really afraid and screamed, "Help! I'm being chased by Jerry!" We had to rescue her.

Keith Coppen, June's son, used to do a lot of game catching. He was quite a character. He flew in the Rhodesian Air force (now Zimbabwe). He was very daring and had been shot at many times. He was a phenomenal pilot. Once, while on a game capturing flight, Ian and Keith had an engine out. Keith landed in a Marula tree and they all survived. One day Keith came to visit and landed just behind Ian's house. He was so drunk that he actually fell out of his helicopter. He lay on the ground and Jerry came up to him. Keith looked up and said, "Hi Jerry! How are you?"

He put his hands around Jerry's head and was lifted up into the air. Keith, being drunk, couldn't hold on and he fell to the ground. Ian said, "I really hope that has sobered you up, Keith, because, if not, there's no way that you're flying this helicopter out."

Keith replied, "No, no, I have just popped in for a beer. That will sober me up sufficiently."

He went inside and helped himself to a beer, drank it, jumped into the helicopter and got ready to fly off. Much concerned, Ian asked, "Keith, how the hell do you know where you're flying if you're so drunk?" Said Keith, "This helicopter knows its way home." And off he flew to Mica where he was living at that time.

Months later, while doing a capture on Rhino at another game farm, Keith had an accident and crashed, breaking his neck. We were sorry to lose such a wonderful friend.

When Keith was killed June was playing bridge at The Coach House. It was terribly sad. His father was on a banana farm in Tzaneen and was walking in the plantation when he heard on the radio that his son had been killed.

Mark, another close friend of Chris's, had only one leg. He also studied in Pretoria at the same time as Chris. In spite of his handicap, or perhaps because of it, he lived life to the full. He had lost his leg in a motorbike accident. His leg had been broken, and due to negligence, it had got gangrene and had to be amputated. This had made him very rebellious and he had run away from the hospital four times. Each time they found him and took him back. His way of dealing with his troubles was to choose the worst hot-spots of the terrorist war. He eventually worked through his trauma and decided to go into conservation where he met up with Chris and Les.

One day while Ian, Les and Mark were having lunch they heard Jerry take off down the road. They didn't know what was happening. A member of the game capture crew had decided he wanted to see if he could ride on Jerry. Les and Keith had previously tried to see how long they could remain on Jerry, but the animal had kicked and bucked them off. Mark, with only one leg, climbed on a pole and jumped onto his back when Jerry came past. Jerry allowed him to have a ride and then had let him off gently. Having seen this the member of the crew decided that he, too, would try to have a ride. He copied Mark's strategy, got onto the pole and when the giraffe came past jumped onto Jerry's back. Jerry took off at great speed and the guy got such a fright that he thought the giraffe would never stop and decided to bale off and landed on the ground very hard. He was winded. Served him right!

The filming of *Jock of the Bushveld* took place partly at Tshukudu. One day the crew had the day off and, as they had been having problems with the dog 'Jock'. The dog trainers and an actor, Jonathan Rand, decided to use the day for some practice. They drove the wagon from just below the lodge towards the house dam and back again and the dog had to walk with Jonathan. My friend, Rosemary, who had been helping with the catering, and I were sitting and watching the performance. We saw the wagon and Jonathan walking with the dog and behind them Jerry, the kudu (also known as 'Ronnie Reagan'), the sable ('Pik Botha') and the warthog ('Maggie Thatcher') walking behind the wagon (more about these other animals later). The wagon turned around and came back and all four animals followed. What an amazing sight!

The film company stayed at Tshukudu for 10 days. When they were to move to another venue they asked me to do all the catering while they were filming in the area. I ignored them as we were very short staffed and it involved a lot of work. They then went to Rosemary and begged her to talk me into it. I said to Rosemary, "Go away. I don't want to hear about it."

She said, "Oh go on, Ala! I'll help you. Please. Duncan would love you to carry on especially as there are quite a lot of vegetarians and they loved the menus you provided." She persisted until I eventually gave in. For the rest of the time they were filming, which was about a month, we prepared the food and took it to wherever they were busy shooting.

Sadness and a wedding

Sylvia and her friend, Heidi, were two Swiss girls. They approached me at the Nelspruit office. They were visiting South Africa on holiday and had come in to book a trip to the Kruger National Park. I told them that I could give them a tour with a group of Germans going to the Park, having lunch at Tshukudu and then on to the Blyde River Canyon. They didn't want to go to the Canyon because they had already walked that trail and they just wanted to go to the Park. So I made a suggestion: "I have a good idea for you. You go to the Park with the tour group and Lolly, my husband will be the tour driver." Lolly used to help when we were short of guides. "Go to Tshukudu for the lunch and I will be there," I said, "and I will be travelling back to Nelspruit and could give you a lift there on the same day." They quickly agreed.

As usual I went to Tshukudu with a group of friends to cook and serve the lunch. We ate our lunch underneath the big tree – at that time we had no verandah. Ian and Les Carlisle were at lunch that day. Suddenly Sylvia said, "I don't think that we will be going back to Nelspruit today."

I asked, "Have you decided to go to the Canyon after all?"

"No," replied Sylvia, "Your husband has invited us to stay here for a bit." Needless to say my suspicions were aroused! I suspected that their chief incentive for staying was not just to see more of Tshukudu, but to be able to spend a little more time in the company of Ian and Les. So I left without them.

Les Carlisle took a shine to Heidi, an attractive little lass. He suggested to Ian that they should take the girls out on their bikes in order to show them a capture. Ian was very shy and did not consider ladies to be part of his set up. This ride, however, was the beginning of many more pleasurable outings including a moonlit drive. So the romance developed. Unknown to me at that time, Ian even showed Sylvia where they could build their house one day. It all went very fast. The two girls had developed a love for animals, among other things, and so they stayed on at Tshukudu and enjoyed game viewing from the back of motorbikes.

From Tshukudu the girls travelled to Zimbabwe. I invited them to return to the farm for Christmas to which they readily agreed. Eventually they had to go back to Switzerland where Sylvia wasted no time in obtaining a work permit for South Africa and eventually returned. Once back in South Africa she registered for the compulsory six month's nursing course which would allow her training to be recognised in order to work in South African hospitals. I was still in Nelspruit so we often travelled together to Tshukudu. Later she bought a little Volkswagen Beetle which gave her independence.

After Sylvia returned to South Africa she and Ian were able to get to know each other better. She spent as much time as possible at Tshukudu and the two had great fun including tubing down a river passing beautiful pools, crocodiles and hippos.

One day Sylvia and I were at Tshukudu, but we had travelled in separate cars. I suggested she could return with me. This didn't suit her plans, however, as she wanted to stay on a little longer. Driving back on her own I think she fell asleep at the wheel of her little VW Beetle and it overturned. Fortunately, she was not hurt but the car was badly damaged. Ian was on a six month's mechanical course in Bloemfontein at the time. He had been reluctant to go because it meant leaving Sylvia, but I was sure that the course would stand him in good stead as we were dependent on generators at Tshukudu, and they had a tendency to break down, and there were always vehicles in need of repair. As part of his practical examination Ian chose to repair Sylvia's car. He did a good job on it and passed well. Perhaps this was a true labour of love. They went over to Switzerland to meet her family and, knowing how shy Ian was, Sylvia said, "Seeing as we're here perhaps you should ask my parents if you can marry me." So they got engaged and on their return to South Africa began their wedding preparations.

When Ian and Sylvia declared their intentions to get married I decided to move to Tshukudu once and for all. We now had regular tours to Tshukudu from Nelspruit and decided to build another rondawel. The cost of the building in those days was about R8 000. I also borrowed R7 000 to put up a fence between our property and the part on the other side of the railway line that we had sold. We still had enormous debt so we sold another part of the property to pay it off. Finally we were out of debt. But our income was quite small once I had given up my job in Nelspruit.

We lived in Nelspruit for a total of 10 years before we bought the farms and in 1983 three years later, eventually, spurred on by the forthcoming wedding, I moved to the new place full time.

When I left Nelspruit, Mother had moved into an old age home but she spent a lot of time at Tshukudu. One evening when she was staying with us I had planned that two of our friends should visit us so that we could play bridge. She was not feeling very well and I suggested that she should see a doctor, but she did not think that she was sick enough for that.

The following morning Chris and I went for a walk and I popped in to see her. She said that she was much better and really looking forward to our evening of bridge. She went out to pick flowers. She returned to the lodge carrying the flowers and suddenly fell down. Lolly carried her to a bed but when I returned I was given the sad news – she had passed away. She had suffered a heart attack. She had been so excited about Ian's wedding which was only four weeks away.

Ala's Story

She had even planned her dress. Although she was 78 years old, she was still an amazing woman. Everybody loved her, but her life had been hard. For me she was always a role model but I'm afraid that I am a bit materialistic, which she never was. I need to know that I have money to live comfortably in the future. She would give everything she possessed to others that she felt were more needy. She was a saint. She had wanted to be buried on Tshukudu, but all her friends and her priest were in Nelspruit so we got a permit and took her body to Nelspruit and buried her there.

At the time there were people staying at Tshukudu but I was in no fit state to look after them so Anne and Tony Morgan came in to help us.

The morning of the funeral Lesley and Mark arrived. They looked terrible – Khaki scruffy clothing and slip-slops, with black ties around their necks. I was aghast! How could they attend a funeral like that? They said, "This is the way Babcia would have wanted us to be." However, they were only joking in an attempt to lift my spirits and changed before the funeral.

At the funeral Lesley, Ian's friend, spoke so beautifully about Mother. He referred to her as his adopted granny. This is certainly a person about whom I could talk for hours. She had suffered so much. She was deported to Siberia as a student and then again as a mother. She lost her husband for 18 years – all the tragedies which played such a huge role in her life but which never embittered her. She was always so positive.

Jerry helping himself to the decorations on the jeep

I felt that it would not serve any purpose to cancel the wedding. The invitations had all been sent out and Sylvia's family had booked their flights to come to South Africa. I also felt that Babcia would have liked the wedding to proceed as planned. She was one of the most unselfish people that I have known. Goodbye, Mother, we miss you.

So the wedding took place. It was certainly a different kind of wedding. We decided to decorate the jeep, which was a very special one, in which Sylvia was to travel with bougainvillaea, but as fast as we put the flowers on the vehicle so Jerry ate them.

Sylvia arrived in the vehicle with her father. We had made an altar at the side of the big tree, with a carpet of animal skins leading up to it.

Our priest from Nelspruit came to officiate at the ceremony. The wedding was lovely. There were about 60 guests. Jerry walked around, chickens, birds and squirrels completed the picture. It was unbelievable with such a happy atmosphere.

It was also the occasion of their first argument! Sylvia kept turning around to look at the animals. She was distracted by all the activity of chickens, dogs and children. Ian rather irritably whispered to her, "Forget about the animals and

Sylvia's parents, Trudi and Hans, Heidi, Sylvia, Ian, me, Lolly, Lolly's mom, Chris, and Janusz's daughter, Tanya

Ala's Story

concentrate on what the priest is saying!" Sylvia was justifiably cross.

Sylvia's father and mother, Hans and Trudie, plus her brother, Werner, and his former wife, as well as her uncle and aunt all attended the wedding. Ian's friends all wore black arm bands in memory losing a friend. Les was master of ceremonies, and with his gift for making speeches charmed and entertained us. Janusz had unfortunately already left for Australia, so he was unable to attend.

In the beginning we had all lived in the house. We really didn't have the money to build anything else but eventually began to build our house. We made the bricks ourselves and it was a very slow process.

Once they were married I decided that Ian and Sylvia should have the little house that we had built for ourselves. It seemed that it would be right for the newlywed couple to have a place of their own.

Some time after the wedding I needed extra staff and decided to employ a chef. A man I will call Sam applied for the post. In order to assess his abilities I asked him to cook a Sunday lunch for the family. It was dreadful. He couldn't cook. He then suggested that I should give him a job as a ranger. He was desperate for work and I felt really sorry for him so I thought I would give him a chance.

One day we were to have a bush dinner around a fire at the dam. Sam went ahead in order to organise the fire. Chris was to join us later with his clients. As their plane had been delayed we didn't expect them until about 10pm. We all went to the dam and enjoyed our evening. We had finished eating when Chris arrived with his guests. We were already packing up the stuff so I offered the guests some wine to enjoy around the fire. I then set off for the lodge to organise dinner for the late arrivals. I told Sam to leave the wine for the guests who would follow later. A short way towards the lodge I asked Sam if he had left a bottle opener. He said he hadn't so I said, "Okay! I'll wait here for you while you run down to the party. It won't take you more than five minutes."

We waited and we waited. Sam had taken a wrong turn and was running towards the main gate. Eventually we realised what had happened and had to go in search of him.

Sam was so keen to prove himself that he would rush from the boma in the evening to fetch a bottle of wine from the bar – a distance of some 50 meters. One day in his hurry he hit a tree branch. Chris came out of the boma and saw him lying on the ground with the wine bottle, unbroken, still in his hand. He was so proud that he had saved the wine.

One day we sent him to let the blinds down in one of the cottages. We had a fence around it because Jerry used to rummage in the thatch. Sam opened the gate and at that moment lightening struck. He was thrown to the ground, smoke rising from his body. He was really lucky to be alive and relatively unhurt. Chris found him lying there and asked what had happened. Sam replied, "I really don't know but, gee, I'm smoking!"

Once, before we had sufficient accommodation, we were using a neighbouring ranch for a couple of our guests. I told Sam to collect them for lunch. 2pm came and went and still no Sam. He had been driving around the property, completely lost. The guests had a prolonged game drive, but arrived very hungry.

To give him his due, he had determination. He bought a computer and books on animals and learnt so much that his knowledge of animals was tops. But I couldn't help laughing at him. He was an accident waiting to happen.

I need to complete the story of Jerry. Shortly after he turned five he was attacked by lions and they broke his leg and he had to be put down. It was a Christmas day. We really missed him. We missed him on our walks when he used to lag behind and then we would hear him galloping in order to catch up. We would have to be careful because he would come at quite a speed and could easily knock a person over. We all loved him very much. My mother once said, "Jerry understood when I was sad because when I felt unhappy he came and licked me."

Adventure in the bush

Ian started school camps and adventure trips. An example of one of his adventure trips was when he took a group of senior boy scouts on such an adventure – three days on the river and two days tracking elephant. They certainly had some adventures. They were chased by hippos and encountered crocodiles which surfaced in the tube on the raft. They had to porter around the hippo pools which made the days very long.

When they first started their school camps all they had was a boma in the bush with a shower and a water tank. It was really wild. The children slept in the boma. The first group that came was from a convent in Nelspruit and they have subsequently returned every year for the past quarter-century. Another time we had a school from Johannesburg with a teacher called Jenny.

We had a little hand-reared duiker called Tshukudu. It was a delightful animal but when a duiker male grows up it can get very cheeky. This one used to chase everyone. He hated Les Carlisle. Duiker have very sharp little horns and can cause a lot of damage. Les was actually terrified because once he'd had a duiker horn in his leg which had been very painful. Every time he arrived here he would ask where Tshukudu was.

On this particular school visit Jenny was sitting with us when a little girl came running up, "Teacher, teacher! Tshukudu the duiker is chasing all the girls."

"That's nonsense!" said Jenny but she went to the boma where she found all the girls sitting on the bar counter. Somewhat annoyed, Jenny demanded to know what they thought they were doing. With that the duiker attacked her so she joined the 30 girls on top of the bar. Ian had to go to their rescue. The little animal had a school bag caught around his neck which had made him even more agitated.

When we first moved here we met the Craigs. They used to have church services in their home before there was a proper church. One day Anne Craig came to visit with a friend. By that time we had two rondawels and Anne asked if she could show one to her friend. They were gone for absolute ages and I started to be worried about them. So I went to look for them. Tshukudu was standing outside the door of one of the rondawels so I called out to ask if they were inside. Anne replied, "We're trapped. Tshukudu won't let us out!"

"Nonsense!" I responded. I tried to chase Tshukudu away but he turned on me. I jumped inside the rondawel. There were now three of us being held prisoner by a duiker! In those days we didn't have cellphones or radios. I asked Anne to go to the door and try to distract Tshukudu while I jumped through the side window and ran for help.

Philip Lategan had been my boss after we sold our Nelspruit business and I was

Lolly, Sonja and Chris with Shumba

still working there. He was based in Johannesburg at the head office of Magnum Airlines. Once he came to stay with us on the farm. One beautiful moonlit night we decided to walk down to the dam – the first little dam near the house. There had been rain and I wanted to check on how much water there was in it. We were standing at the dam, Philip right near the edge, when out of the bush came Tshukudu and bumped Philip from behind. He landed on his back in a rather undignified manner. I have to say that I was secretly a little bit happy, because Philip was rather conceited. After this, not because of it, Tshukudu disappeared for about six months. We didn't know what had happened to him and wondered if he'd been taken by lion. One day Lolly was taking a group for a game drive when he saw a duiker and thought it might be Tshukudu. He stopped the vehicle, called to the duiker and climbed down from the driver's seat. It was Tshukudu and he ran over to Lolly, licked him and then ran back into the bush. The guests couldn't believe it. It was a touching story. The little buck remembered Lolly. We never saw him again.

Lolly, Ian, Chris and myself did all the work at the lodge. We pampered the guests and attended to all their needs. After the boys got married there was a need to establish each of the boys in his own business. This would prevent any friction about the amount of time each of the them put in. They never always agreed and there were confrontational situations. They wanted their own time. So we decided it would be best if each person took a department, ran it and took responsibility for it. Ian took over the bush camp which now consisted of a platform and two cottages.

We were also starting a little hunting safari business – no shooting here, but organising other venues. Chris took over that part. He gradually built up the camp which was a good thing as it is difficult to mix people who shoot with guns with those that shoot with cameras. Hunters want to talk about their experiences and the photographic people don't want to hear about them. Chris built his home and put up the tents. Sonja, Chris's wife, decorated their home – and camp – beautifully.

Remembering the safaris Chris says, "The main flow of money from game was through hunting. When the Rand was weak, hunting took off. Lots of people came in and there was a lot of harvesting so the turnover was quite good. Now the Rand is stronger there are fewer hunters so the turnover is slow – the demand is slow. Bureaucracy is also making it more difficult to get people on a hunt."

The only hunting we do here is when an animal has been injured or becomes a danger. We also need to pay attention to numbers. For example, we now have a surplus of buffalo bulls as a result of capturing a lot of the cows. The situation is unbalanced. We have about a 150 which is too many for the area. Chris may use clients for this to generate some income to plough back into conservation. He goes overseas to promote his venture. He also takes clients to other concessions and areas where they can hunt.

The tented camp is also used out of hunting season as a self-catering holiday place. This is necessary as it would not be economical for it to remain empty for such long periods of time.

Chris met Sonja when she was a representative for a company that advertised game reserves. They were married and were together for ten years. Sonja took a few orphaned animals under her wing and was a big help in the running of the camp. They had a happy marriage until things went sour.

The two of them are still good friends. He's a really good father to his children,

Matthew, Chris and Jessica

Matthew and Jessica who are moggy over wildlife. Chris thinks that his son would also like to have a career related to wildlife, but he is determined that they should follow their own hearts.

Of course, I still love Sonja. She's a lovely girl and I was very sad when their marriage broke up. She's the mother of my grandchildren and it was terrible when she walked out of our lives.

Ian and Sylvia built up their business together. Obviously once the babies started to come Sylvia stayed at home but was still active in the running of the camp. They now have four boys, Patrick, David, Steven and Richard. Sylvia still does a lot of work for the bush camp – buying, booking and catering, picking up and dropping off children. The camp caters for schools and overseas students as well as offering affordable self-catering facilities for South Africans.

The farm at Ohrigstad was originally bought when we were experiencing a terrible drought and we were desperate for fodder for our animals which was exorbitantly expensive and often unavailable. On the farm we could grow our own lucerne and it would work out much cheaper. We grow a lot of lucerne there so we are able to stockpile and in the event of another drought we have fodder for the animals. We pay a lot to keep the place going but it will even out in the end. It is kept as a place where family can go to get away from everything. We have had problems there with managers. Our first was a young student and he used to invite his friends there and they would go out at night shooting the game indiscriminately. Another one also took people hunting. The place has been developed and fenced off which was a huge task. We have also stocked it with a huge amount of game.

Steven, David, Ian, Sylvia, Richard and Patrick (with bee-stung face)

Ala's Story

A close shave

In the early days I used to do all the shopping in the town of Phalaborwa. One day I needed to go and didn't have a vehicle suitable for all the things I wanted to buy. Lolly has always been very protective about his vehicles and resists lending them out, even to family. This day I really had to beg him to let me use his *bakkie* (pick up truck). He agreed and off I went accompanied by a ranger whose task it was to obtain some licences. I parked in Phalaborwa in a safe place in a supermarket parking area. While busy with my purchases I happened to walk past the bakkie several times. I was most surprised when the ranger came running to me and said that the *bakkie* was gone.

"Nonsense!" I said, "I saw it a few minutes ago."

He persuaded me to go and look and it was true.

I went to the manager of the supermarket and asked him to contact the police and suggested that they put up road blocks on the three exit roads out of Phalaborwa, to Namakgale, to Tzaneen and to Hoedspruit. The police were most helpful but I was a nervous wreck. What would Lolly say? Anyway I had to phone him in order to get transport back to Tshukudu. I said, "I'm really sorry but your *bakkie* has been stolen. Please will you come and collect me but keep a lookout for the vehicle because it could be coming in your direction."

Our friend, Seun, from Swaziland, was staying with us at the time so he and Lolly climbed into his *kombi* (van) and set off. They had only passed the border of Tshukudu when Lolly spied his *bakkie* coming towards them with an unmarked sedan in close pursuit. Lolly wanted to jump out of the kombi but Seun persuaded him that it would be dangerous. They turned around and followed the stolen vehicle. The chap in the sedan was a member of the CID but was really worried when he saw he was between the stolen car and what he thought were accomplices in the vehicle with Swaziland number plates. The thief saw he was being followed by two cars and he panicked. He stopped the *bakkie*, jumped out and took off into the bush on the side of the road with the CID behind him. In his haste he ran into a fence and fell into a ditch. Lolly followed firing his rifle into the air. It must have had all the makings of a true 'Wild West'. The bakkie had been stolen by a syndicate based in Pretoria. Our thief would not talk so they kept him locked up but the police were eventually able to break up the syndicate.

More animal escapades

Ian, Chris and their friends had so many adventures at Tshukudu, mostly involving animals. Mark used to go with Ian on crocodile hunts in order to stock our dams. They would ride down to the river on their bikes. The river was on the property of a friend called Bruce. He would hold the torch (flashlight) while the other two caught the crocodiles. Once, when they were chased by a hippo and had to run to safety, Ian remembers, "I ran as fast as I could and couldn't believe my eyes when Mark passed me on crutches. This made me realise that the hippo was dangerously close and I needed to run for my life. Mark dropped his torch and stopped to retrieve the batteries, but thought better of it when he realised that the hippo was breathing down his neck."

Shortly after the hippo incident the three saw a crocodile lying on a sand bank in the middle of the river. Mark and Bruce aimed their torches at the crocodile in order to blind it. Ian crept up as quietly as possible so as not to alert the creature. The slightest noise would have sent the croc into deep water and they would not have been able to capture it. While stalking along in the water Ian disturbed a hippo. The two fellows on the bank saw a huge splash and thought Ian had been taken by a crocodile. Meanwhile Ian had leapt up the bank to safety. He was quite shocked but the others had not seen him. He walked up to the two and tapped them on the shoulders. They thought he was a ghost and jumped about as high as Ian had. They then decided that they had better go home but needed a short rest to recover from the night's exertions. They sat on a rock, close to the river. Unknown to them, a hippo was submerged close by and needed to take a breath. He leapt out of the water nearly over Mark's head. That was it – time to go home.

Another time, when they were going out crocodile catching, they invited a British tourist to join them. Bruce fetched them in his Land Rover, an open vehicle that offered little protection. It had been raining but it was a lovely bright night. When they stopped they saw a big pride of lions. This did not concern them as they were concentrating on the crocodile hunt. Their British guest was appalled, saying, "There are lions out there!" The boys said, "Yes, this is Africa." The man was very nervous. He was anxious about getting out of the vehicle but did not want to stay alone in it. He decided that it would be safer with the others but when he saw the water he wanted to know whether or not there were crocodiles in it.

"Of course!" responded Ian "That's what we're here for."

Bruce stayed with the guest. He had a shot gun which did make the British chap feel a little more secure. He still, however, repeatedly scoured the whole surrounding area looking for lions, hippos or any sign of crocodiles. They saw eyes emerge above the water and thought they had found their first crocodile. Mark and Ian decided to stalk it. It turned out to be a hippo. When they realised their mistake they gave the creature a wide berth and went back to the rest of the party. The dogs had disappeared – probably chased by the lions, so they decided to go and look for them. They all climbed into the Land Rover and saw the pride as they rounded a corner. Mark decided to go after the lions on his crutches. Unfortunately he tripped on the uneven surface of the road and the lions immediately saw 'food'. Ian and Bruce were just in time to rescue both Mark and the dogs.

After their marriage, Sylvia made Ian promise never to go crocodile hunting again.

Gaining friends, animals and space

Gradually our business grew. We had some help from a South African women's magazine, *Fair Lady*, which published an article about the lodge and proved to be an excellent promotion.

We also began to increase out animal population. We started off by acquiring four rhinos. The name Tshukudu means rhino in two of our 11 official languages – Tswana and Northern Sotho. As the rhinos were among our first imported animals, it was most appropriate that we honoured them with our name. At that time Princess Di and Prince Charles were celebrating their marriage and two of the rhinos seemed to be very much in love so we named them Charles and Di. The other pair of rhinos were always fighting so friends named them Lolly and Ala because they said we were always scrapping. Lolly and Ala were quite a worry when they escaped from the farm. We were in the middle of a drought and the farmer on to whose land they strayed was quite short with us when he requested that we get them off his farm as quickly as possible as he was very short of water. We had a problem capturing them as Blackie Swart's helicopter was in for repairs, and we were forced to resort to darts.

We found a big truck and finally managed to return them to Tshukudu. This time we decided to put the pair into the capture boma before releasing them into the wilds. Pat French and I sat chatting while waiting for the truck to arrive. On their arrival the driver reversed the truck into the boma and they tried to pull the rhinos out by their tails. The obstinate animals refused to budge. When they eventually came out it was with a tremendous rush and I've never seen so many fat, thin, short and tall men scatter with such alacrity. They took cover anywhere they could – under the truck and up trees. Pat and I were hysterical with laughter. The recalcitrant rhinos were eventually released and they still wander happily in Tshukudu. They got so tame that we could walk up to them and touch and scratch them. It was so incredible to see wild animals that had got used to us. We found that when we were feeding them in times of drought that they were very docile, but when the rains came they wandered back into the bush and reverted to their wild state, which is what we want. They tolerate us but if one starts snorting it's telling you not to get too close. If you don't heed the warning it could provoke a charge. We have subsequently sold one of the males from the original lot that we bought. They've had many babies and each year we sell about two. We paid R1 000 per rhino for the original lot, and in 2004 we sold at R175 000 per rhino. We sold one of our males and bought another in order to introduce new blood into our rhino population. Now the price has gone down and we would probably only get about R75 000 each. But the rhinos are still a good investment when one thinks about their original cost a quarter-century ago. Rhinos don't mate for life. Usually one needs two bulls in a herd to ensure successful breeding.

At one time Nature Conversation used to send out rangers to patrol on bicycles to help prevent poaching. They would load their bicycles with all their requirements such as green sails and anything else they would need in order to sleep in the bush. It was a time of severe drought so we were feeding the rhino with lucern. We would place the bales in front of the lodge and were able to watch the animals coming to eat. One day while watching the rhino we noticed two conservation rangers on their bikes riding past. The rhino noticed the green sails on the back of the bikes and must have thought it was more lucern, so they went towards the guys on their bikes. The two rangers took off at speed, pedalling as fast as they could. The faster they went, the faster ran the rhino. Eventually the two men threw their bikes down and took off on foot. Of course, the rhinos stopped in order to investigate the green packs, so it took quite a bit of time to retrieve those bikes!

Gradually we added to our buildings. We built chalets three and four. An architect friend said that we were crazy building rondawels. He felt that they were a waste of space and money. He was right in that there is less space in a circular house – at least in terms of placing furniture. I should never have listened to him because the round buildings are cooler and have greater appeal for the tourists. However, we heeded his advice and put up buildings with two rooms instead of rondawels. One day I would like to change our buildings, especially as the market has now become very competitive although we are not selling accommodation per se, but a bush experience. When we first bought the farm the only other game lodges were Motswari, Ngala and Madumba Boma. They had tents and little chalets. Now there are many game lodges in the area. Everyone is trying to outdo the others but I think we will work at maintaining our ethos.

Work here never ends. People don't realise all the things we have to do. We need to maintain the buildings as well as the bush, care for the animals and look after any orphans with the aim of re-introducing them to the wild.

Anecdotes

With increasing trade I employed a chef named Judas. A friend in Nelspruit sent him to me and he arrived for his interview immaculate, dressed in white shoes, a white uniform and all the right touches. He certainly looked grand. However, he took one look at the bush and said that there was no way he could live here. So we suggested that he live in a room we'd build for him near the house. He agreed to stay and proved to be a great help until one day I discovered that Judas was an alcoholic. All of my brandy puddings were without brandy; all my sherry puddings were sans sherry. He worked for me for a while but one Easter weekend he decided he needed a break. He took off for the day knowing that I would need him back on the following day to help out with a school group and some German clients who were staying at the lodge. The school group was sleeping in the bush boma but still needed to be fed. Judas chose this time not to return to work and to make matters worse, I had flu. In the meantime I had met a lady named Beauty who was a friend of Judas. Beauty had been working for friends of mine in White River but they had sold their farm and she was out of work. Because I had already employed Judas, I didn't have a vacancy for her although she impressed me. I asked a friend, Jane Mathews, if she needed help at the Magoebaskloof Hotel. She did, and that's where Beauty found employment.

Another friend, June Coppen, told me about the bridge school that had been started at The Coach House Hotel, near Tzaneen, and suggested I might like to join. It was here that I met many new friends such as Gael, who was married to a good friend of ours from Northern Rhodesia, Peter Williamson. When Judas did not pitch up for work I turned to Lolly and said, "You must go to the Magoebaskloof Hotel and fetch Beauty. I am too ill to cope here on my own."

I phoned the hotel and asked Beauty if she would be able to come here and when would be a good time for her. She said, "Tonight!"

Lolly decided that he would have dinner with Gael and Peter who lived on a farm not far from the hotel, and then fetch Beauty at about 10pm. What a relief it was for me to see her. Even feeling so ill I still had to cook dinner for our German guests, but it was so good to have Beauty take over. She is still with me, more than 20 years later.

Another loyal employee I'd like to mention is Lamson. He was the sole caretaker of the farm when we first took over. He is still with us. And then there's Orlando, our chief caterer, who we've known since he was a small child. He arrived as a refugee from Mozambique and I personally put him through school to ensure he benefited from a good education; Orlando has since grown into a very talented young gentleman and has become a great asset to Tshukudu. Hilda has also been part of Tshukudu for many years. She makes sure that there is no waste of food. She collects all the leftovers and feeds some porcupines which visitors are privileged to see.

Ala's Story

Animal love affairs

After we purchased the rhino we invested in buffalo. We got a lot of buffalo from neighbouring cattle farms. The animals had wandered onto the farms from the game reserve and the farmers were fearful that the wild animals might be carrying foot and mouth disease. We made a deal with the game capturers and went with them to capture our own buffalo. Foot and mouth disease is not a problem in wild animals, but does cause problems with domestic stock. Being so close to Kruger National Park, where the disease is rampant, we can hardly get rid of it, but because we don't have cattle, we're not too worried. To these original buffalo we added another 25 which we bought. Combined, they were the start of our buffalo population. We also brought in waterbuck, which have done extremely well.

Tshukudu has made a significant contribution towards South African wildlife conservation. We were one of the early pioneers in the game industry and – as a result – we were responsible for the reintroduction of the first giraffe back onto private land in KwaZulu-Natal and also in the Tuli block in southern Botswana. All our surplus animals are captured and sold to re-stock other game farms and reserves throughout the country.

When we started Tshukudu we were totally surrounded by cattle farmers who were very hostile towards predators and wild animals in general. This was understandable as they were protecting their livestock and future. Wild animals have been blamed for transmitting all kinds of diseases to domestic livestock. Some of these allegations were founded – and others not – but, unfortunately, wild animals were used as scapegoats.

At that time, the government was also doing very little to ensure the future survival of predators, in particular lions. Of South Africa's 20 national parks, only three have lions and the Addo National Park (one of the three) only had lions introduced in 2006; there are only eight lions, not really enough to establish a significant population in such a large area. The other two national parks include the Kalahari (including central Botswana) with less than 500 lions, and Kruger, which has around 2 000 lions. Unfortunately, around 80 per cent of Kruger's lions are infected with tuberculosis and could die in the next 10 to 15 years. This will leave us with very few lions in South Africa. If we look at the status of lions on the African continent, the picture isn't much rosier – the population is estimated to be 20 000 to 30 000, which is far too few. Everyone talks about saving elephants but we currently have an pan-African elephant population of around 600 000 – this gives you an idea of the grave situation in which lions find themselves.

Tshukudu started a lion-breeding project in 1985 after we witnessed the rapid decline of lions in our area as a result of cattle farmers destroying all of the lions that had moved out of the Kruger National Park. We approached the relevant authorities to gain the necessary permits and – after much persuasion – permission was finally granted to capture problem lions that were killing livestock on the Park's western boundaries. No single individual or organisation has made a bigger contribution towards the future of lions in South Africa – something which we're very proud about. The lion project grew over the years and we were responsible for the reintroduction of lions into most of the country's private game reserves. Even more significantly, ours are only one of two South African lion populations free of tuberculosis – and the only true southern lions.

TB broke out in Kruger in the mid-1980s as a result of buffalo that had crossed the Crocodile River, contracting TB from infected cattle. It spread very rapidly among the buffalo population, as they congregate in large herds and, in turn, lions contracted TB through their preying on buffalo. As a result, the entire southern lion population is now threatened. TB also affects leopard and cheetah, but they're

A young Shumba with an orphan zebra, Zebby

Ala's Story

not pride-based animals and they don't kill buffalo (the main carriers of TB).The unfortunate part of all this? People are very unaware of the dangers that TB poses to Southern African lions. The end result? Very little lobbying for action from the general public to get the government to change its policy and become proactive.

The government, in the meantime, has closed down all lion breeding projects as a result of bad publicity from the canned lion-hunting saga.

Ian provides the background: "A 'canned' lion is a captive, or bred, lion that's released onto a game farm, or enclosed area, to be hunted. The government's requirements for a hunt to take place was that the area had to be at least 1 000 hectares (although size varied from province to province). When this industry was exposed by the Cooke Report an immense amount of damage was done to South Africa's conservation image. As a result, the government decided to clamp down on all lion breeding projects in the country as there's no doubt that most of the lion breeders were involved in breed-to-hunt projects, which is very unfortunate. We also brought it to the authorities' attention that many lions were being imported into South Africa from other African countries, as well as from circuses and zoos around the world – and they were seriously contaminating our pure Southern African lion population, which we were trying to protect and re-establish throughout the country.

Unfortunately, certain people were making big money out of breeding lions for canned shooting – this was the direct result of poor government regulation and the lack of legislation to control the abuse. Ultimately, South African lions will be the losers. Only time will tell whether we made enough of a contribution towards making a difference for the lions of Southern Africa."

'If it pays it stays' is the most important philosophy when it comes to wildlife and conservation. This was made clear to me when we first started. Most cattle farmers in the area used to invite their friends and family to visit and hunt wild animals – for free – on their own property. When animals acquired a 'value' the attitude of cattle farmers quickly changed. This created a win-win situation benefiting the conservation of wild animals and a profitable return for the farmers. The saddest part is seeing the potential and value of our wild animals only when money's involved. Still, we're very happy to report that game farms today are worth five times more than the value of cattle farms – as a result, the land utilisation in our area today has shifted to 98 per cent game farm.

There are 8 000 game farmers in South Africa today – with 14-million hectares under conservation (in comparison: the massive, world-famous Kruger, which has a 'mere' 2-million hectares). There has never been as many animals as there are now in South Africa, or such a large part of our land dedicated to conservation – and it's very encouraging for the future.

We have had our share of incidents with lions in the breeding camps. Once, a

Shumba

wild lion managed to get into one of the camps after part of the fence had been broken by an elephant. We wanted to dart it but had problems in locating it. Eventually Chris and Ian went in and they saw it lying under a tree. They shot it with a dart gun but on impact the dart just disintegrated and with the commotion the other lions were attracted. The wild lion was in a bad state as it had been hounded and attacked by the residents of the camp. Ian and Chris couldn't give chase with the vehicle because of the thick bush, so they had to go in on foot. They managed to separate the lions and the intruder who ran into a fence. He felt cornered and chased Chris. Ian covered Chris with his pistol, but the confused lion suddenly turned and went after Ian.

In those days the boys were quite fit and could run. I'm sure they broke all land speed records in their effort to evade the angry and terrified lion. While fleeing Ian turned around to see where the creature was and was horrified to realise it was so close to him that he could practically reach out and touch it. The lion was set on revenge and determined to take Ian out. He spun around with his .44 magnum revolver in hand and realised that he would have to shoot it or be killed. Ian didn't want to kill the beast so aimed his shot to one side of the head, so the bullet wouldn't go into the brain. The lion went down. Chris ran up demanding to know why Ian had shot the lion – he didn't seem too concerned about the danger his brother had been in. As they were arguing the lion got to its feet and took off into the bush. The boys were relieved. They called out the vet, caught the injured lion, treated it and it lived. Eventually it was released into the wild.

Shumba was one of the original lions that was hand-raised by Sonja and Chris. We had such fun with him. When Chris was building his house he would regularly go to check on its progress and Shumba would follow. When the labourers saw them coming they would take off – into the scaffolding, trees or any other high place. They were petrified of this lion. Shumba thought it a big joke and loved to chase them when they ran away. He, too, could climb trees! When the second floor of the building had been started Chris, followed by Shumba, climbed the stairs to take a look. The poor chap working on this section ran along one of the beams and, of course, Shumba followed. In fear the worker jumped all the way down to escape what he thought would be an instant and painful death.

One day I was in the office talking on the phone and a salesman arrived in his little car. He climbed out of the car and donned his jacket, preening himself in preparation to impress. He started walking around the side of the building towards the verandah. As he turned the corner he saw Shumba lying there. He couldn't make up his mind as to whether the lion was wild or tame but decided that discretion would be the best policy, so he started to back off. Of course, when

Shumba, a star of 'Jock of the Bushveld'

Shumba saw the guy he followed. The pace of the retreat got considerably faster until the poor salesman was at full speed with Shumba after him. The unfortunate man managed to find safety in his little car. Shumba jumped onto the bonnet and observed his quarry through the windowscreen. It looked as if he was thinking, "What the hell were you running away from?"

The poor guy was white with fear. One of the rangers went out to rescue him and take him to the verandah, but he had completely forgotten what he had planned to say. He sat there shaking. Shumba came and sat next to him and started chewing on his briefcase. We tried to stop him, but the man said, "No! Just let him."

Lolly and I often went for walks in the evening. We used to go towards the fence where the lion camps are now situated. Shumba often followed us. One day there were people working on the railway line. Suddenly we heard shouting and screaming. The workers were shouting at us in their own language, which we didn't understand. Finally it dawned on us that they were shouting something like, "There's a lion behind you. Run!" They thought we were being stalked by a wild lion.

Shumba was the lion that appeared in the film *Jock of the Bushveld*. He's 'shot' in the film. Naturally he wasn't really injured, and had to be drugged so that when he was shot it looked realistic. While he was sleeping they painted a bullet hole on his head with red paint to look like blood. In the making of the film they used

Sunshine allows Ian to pet her while she is feeding her cubs

tricks to make it look realistic. For instance, they set up their cameras behind a fence and enticed him to charge. A lion is very possessive of what it's got; for example, a female or food. Meat was placed near the fence and they were able to get the shot. There was always a backup in case any of the animals went bad – something one has to have when dealing with potentially dangerous animals. Everyone who saw the film thought he had really been shot, but he lived up to the ripe old age of 18. In the bush a lion will probably live for ten to eleven years but in camps you can prolong their lives a bit. He died in 2006 and even when he was really old he still occasionally fathered a litter of cubs. He was the leader of his pride. He was a grumpy old man with a little bit of arthritis. He got saggy and his teeth were pretty worn down but he still managed to eat his food and cover females.

Another Shumba story is about South African filmmaker Leon Schuster and his movie *There's A Zulu On My Stoep*. There was a scene of a poacher that they caught. They drugged him and buried his legs. When he came round he found a lion standing over him and he thought that the lion had eaten his legs. A rather cruel trick, but I'm sure it put an end to his poaching activities.

Chris used to go in to the camp with Shumba and allow the fully-grown lion to climb all over him. His knowledge of the ways of lions stood him in good stead. He knew that when a lion takes something in its mouth it becomes his possession and it could become aggressive if one tries to take it away from him. It is a worry. What if he took your hand in his mouth and thought it to be his? That's how an attack could start.

Any big animal is a danger. There have been disastrous incidents with people who have lived with an animal all its life and the animal has turned savage. Look at Sigfield and Roy. They had tigers in their houses and played with these animals. Unexpectedly, one of these animals attacked and killed someone on the stage.

Sunshine was another lion that formed strong bonds with us. She had cubs and allowed Ian to pick up the babies to move her and she followed him meekly like a pussycat, relaxed and trusting.

Many people have the misconception that large cats – lion or leopard – raised by humans are not capable of going out and hunting for itself. Hunting is an instinct that is born in them in the same way that a domestic cat will always enjoy catching birds and mice. The problem that arises is not the ability to return to the wild but the lion's lack of fear of humans. It's also a problem if one considers the sheer size of a grown lion. He may just be happy to see you and leaps onto you. He could break your back or severely injure you and that's where the danger arises.

Let me give you an example: a captive breeding programme decided to release cheetahs from its facilities also experienced problems. The criteria that they chose

A baby leopard cares for a lion cub

for a successful release was as little human contact as possible; cheetahs were released into a large enclosure where they could hunt. Essentially the idea was fine but what they forgot was that they had taken these animals from a secure environment where they had no competition from other predators and placed them into a hostile environment where they had to compete for their food. The leopards, lions, hyenas and wild dogs will steal their kills and treat them as competitors. An animal like Savanna (the cheetah), who has been raised by us, was introduced to other predators at an early age under the supervision of our rangers and she manages to cope very well.

Once we had a call from a friend in Phalaborwa who had a cattle farm. He said he had a lot of lions and wanted us to come and catch them. Ian and Chris loaded up a vehicle and asked a student who was with us at the time to accompany them. On their arrival the friend showed them where the lions had been seen. They tied part of a wildebeest carcass to a tree and hid the vehicle. A pride of lions appeared and they managed to dart a large female. As the drug started to take effect she staggered out of sight. The others, sensing danger, scattered into the grass and the task of locating the drugged lion began. This is where the real danger began, as the boys had to walk in the thick bush with a torch among a large pride of (undarted) lions in their brave attempt to locate the (hopefully sleeping) darted lion. Ian and

Chris found her eventually and managed to load her onto the vehicle. They went back and darted a young male, which they also put onto the back of the Land Rover. On inspection they noticed that one of the lions was lying with his nose against the tail gate and was breathing rather heavily. They asked the student to get hold of its tail and pull it a little bit so that he could breathe easier. The lion, although drugged, is still sensitive to any unexpected movement and the student must have moved suddenly. Because of their sharp reflexes a drugged lion can even bite and if they do they will not let go. When the student pulled its tail the lion reacted with a violent movement which resulted in its becoming airborne. The student thought that his number had come up. He let go of the tail and leapt into the air, did an about turn and ended up on the bonnet of the car. The lion hit the dirt and just lay there. There was no way that Chris and Ian could load the heavy animal on their own and they had to do some quick talking to persuade the student to assist them. After this, they decided that they didn't have space for more than the two they had drugged so headed back home. On their return journey they encountered a cloud burst and the roads flooded. Many cars were stuck in the water. Fortunately for the boys the diesel-driven vehicle had a very high clearance but, even so, the water came over the bonnet and into the back. They were concerned the lions were drowning in the back. The drugs were wearing off and the lions were sitting up. They came to a car that appeared to be stuck and the man in the driver's seat wound down the window as they approached. They asked if they could help. As the lion saw the occupant of the car he gave a great roar. The chap got such a fright that he wound up his window with alacrity. The boys were enjoying themselves, but they were also concerned about their load. They had to stop, creep around the side and administer more drugs into the tails of the lions. On reaching Tshukudu they also succeeded in scaring William, the elderly gate watchman, half to death. After some more hair-raising incidents they eventually managed to get their new lions safely into a camp. The student, however, was close to being a nervous wreck and probably vowed never to get so close to lions again.

Although when stories are told everything sounds like a great adventure, Chris and Ian were often potentially in danger but both are sensible and wise to the ways of animals. Stocking up the camp was hard work, but very rewarding – and the memorable experiences we've endured have had a lasting impression on our lives.

Orphans

We have had so many animals that were orphans and had to be hand-raised. We grew to love each of these creatures. Warthogs may be very ugly, but they are quite appealing and funny. We had many warthogs with names like Winston and Snotty. They make fantastic pets. The problem is that they become powerful and very boisterous. They are not inclined to become very aggressive unless you hit them or push them around, then they can behave badly. Animals that are territorial will fight to protect their territory. Female warthogs only come into season for a short time each year and they don't come into the lodge grounds, so we've never had a problem. A tiny but cheeky warthog was brought to us when we were entertaining some British tourists. One was an antique dealer from London. She looked at the warthog and asked, "Have you named this animal yet? Is it male or female?" When I replied 'female' she responded, "Then I think you should call it Maggie Thatcher."

The lady returned to England and wrote to Margaret Thatcher to tell her that there was a warthog named after her in South Africa. Apparently Mrs Thatcher (as she was at that time) replied to say that she was delighted to have a wild animal named after her. I wonder if she knew what a fully-grown warthog looked like?

At the time when Maggie came to the lodge we also acquired a baby monkey named uMfan (little boy). He and Maggie became quite friendly, they even ate

'Maggie Thatcher'
in all her beauty

Ala's Story

together. One day the elephants had broken the fence between us and another reserve and had come into our reserve. I decided to go with the team to fix the fence thinking that I would be back in time to feed my babies but the work took longer than anticipated. My two orphans must have felt neglected. I rushed home as soon as I could to give them their bottles. When I got there I found uMfan riding on Maggie's back sucking his thumb for comfort. From that time on whenever I went for a walk Maggie would come along with uMfan perched on his back. The little monkey also loved to sit on my shoulder when I watched TV, giving me a little kiss every now and then to remind me he was still there.

One day I saw a tractor returning from the bush and I could see there was an animal with them. I identified it as an hyena. It was in the most appalling condition – full of worms, starving and really sick. After cleaning it up we realised it was blind. Dr Blackie Swart said that malnutrition could have caused the blindness and that there was a possibility he could regain his sight. After some time of tender loving care I was thrilled to see Scruffy (the hyena) jumping over a hosepipe. I realised he could see again. He stayed with us for quite some time. He used to visit bedrooms and come into the boma at dinner time. He joined our evening walks with Maggie and uMfan. Gradually, his visits became fewer and then we only heard his call in the evenings. A happy ending.

At that time politics were very prominent in all the news stories. So we followed the trend and called an orphan kudu Ronald Regan and a sable antelope Pik Botha. The sable and the kudu were very good friends and went everywhere together. The kudu was a little mixed up and thought he should eat grass and the grass feeder thought his diet should consist of leaves so they had serious problems. The sable antelope is often aggressive and Pik used to get stuck into Ronald and give him a good beating. The kudu was a very docile animal. This kudu liked to eat the bougainvillea that grew around the lodge. We had a German guest who was fascinated by the kudu. He kept on pulling on its horns. I went up to him and said, "Look, this is a big animal and could do a lot of damage with those horns. Leave him alone. Don't touch him."

I turned around after the warning and walked off. But the chap thought he would give the horns one more pull so he grabbed the horn and gave it a bit of a tug. One of our rangers was sitting on the steps watching. As the guy pulled the horn the kudu whacked him on the head and gave him a nasty cut. The ranger went up to him and said, "Ja, now you know why it's called a kudu. When it hit you on your head it went ka-doo." The fellow seemed actually to be quite pleased.

The sable eventually went out into the bush. The kudu lived in the wild for a long time and eventually died close to the camp of old age, but we think that the sable may have been taken by either poachers or game capturers as sable is a very expensive animal.

*Me with
a young
Savanna*

Most of the problems we have with animals are people induced. They tend to push their luck. We warn people all the time that these are wild animals and that they need respect. Animals also get cross if they are pushed.

We had a waterbuck that had also appeared in *Jock of the Bushveld*. His name was Willie, but he became a bit of a trial. He attacked some schoolchildren as well as Ian. He had been reared by us but eventually went back into the bush and he stationed himself around the bush camp area. One day Willie challenged Ian at the bush camp. Ian put his son onto a vehicle and in the process Willie struck him on the back of his leg quite close to his butt. Ian ran to one of the rooms and the buck chased him. He didn't want to kill the animal but a short while later the buck chased some of the labourers up a tree and kept them there for quite some time. One of the labourers had run so fast that he even lost his shoes. We realised that this was getting serious and couldn't be allowed to continue. It reached a climax when Ian was out with some young boys on a nature walk and the buck charged them, so he was forced to move it to the farm. Humans were his competition. Waterbuck are very aggressive animals and can easily kill you. Willie was defending his females and considered us as a possible threat. And, because he had been hand raised, he didn't have fear of humans. Because of this, many of the animals that we have raised have been taken to our farm in Ohrigstad. There are few humans there, only family, and there's more control. We are able to keep a check on them.

Charlie the Eland was born at Tshukudu. She was in a very poor condition when we found her. We thought it was an injured baby kudu. Later we realised it was an eland. She grew up here but became a bit of a problem because she loved to eat washing. We really couldn't keep her here so she was also moved to Ohrigstad. With eland one female in the herd is appointed as the nursemaid and for a year or so she looks after all the babies in the herd so when the others go off feeding she stays with the babies. Charlie was appointed the nursemaid at Ohrigstad and was responsible for six or seven babies. The babies go back to their mothers at night. When Charlie was relieved of her task she would go to the house and greet us if we were there. Then she would return to the babies. She was gentle but if one got aggressive towards her she could cause trouble. Once one of our rangers went up to Ohrigstad with a girlfriend and they went for a walk. Charlie loved to follow people and this time was no exception. The pair did not want an eland following them but she refused to be turned away. Eventually they took a stick to her so she chased them up a tree.

Female animals go back into the wild and give no trouble. One such animal is Savanna. She came to us when she was about eight weeks old. She was part of a litter of five and the chances of the mother being able to raise all the cubs was slim so we took her into the lodge. A beautiful little cheetah cub that people said we would never be able to raise because she was already too old. But with perseverance and patience she was following us around like a puppy within two days. She was the only one of the litter that survived. She goes out into the

Janusz with an adult Savanna

bush for days on end but she's still as tame as ever when she sees us. When you approach her she purrs. She loves affection. When she sees a vehicle in the bush she runs up to greet it. She's an amazing animal – one of a kind. We have never known another cheetah like her. She's always gentle, always passive and accepts everyone, even children. She has never attacked anyone although she can be playful. She will run up behind you and pounce, but never hurt you. She has a beautiful life now – the best of both worlds.

Savanna goes out hunting and comes back with blood dripping from her jaws which shows she has made a kill. She then settles on the sofa in the lounge because she seems to want the warmth and comfort of the lodge or perhaps just to be with people.

Savanna knows that if her hunting is unsuccessful she is assured of a good meal from the kitchen. The guests love it when she hitches a ride home from one of the vehicles. She is free to do whatever she likes.

We now have a lion cub called Simba. He is one of Shumba's babies. He was born during a bad storm. The rangers saw the cub in the morning and in the afternoon after the storm they saw that the cub had been washed out of the camp, nearly drowning. The lioness was nowhere to be seen. She had left her cub and wandered off. In a case like this it is pointless to try to get the mother to accept it. If she rejects it once she will not take it back again. So we picked it up, fed it and got it going again. It was touch and go for a while, but it survived. He is quite playful. It seems that when the weather is cool and windy he becomes more frisky.

Another doubtful survivor was a baby leopard who was bitten on the head by

Savanna in the driving seat

My grandson, David, with the young leopard

his father and couldn't walk after birth, but just rolled over. We took the baby to the vet who said that there was a swelling on the brain. Sandy and Ross, our manager and his wife, took it in and reared it with so much love. Eventually the leopard started to stabilize. It was amazing. He is now a beautiful animal and has been released into the reserve.

We have had all sorts of orphans at one time or another. We had a baby zebra once that grew up with wildebeest. We moved them to Orighstad for the simple reason that if we let them loose here they would be ignorant of lion and would probably get killed. The wildebeest was male and could have become a little aggressive while the Zebra also liked to kick so it was in the interest of safety that we moved them from Tshukudu.

If animals are raised together they do seem to form friendships. For example, we once had a leopard, a serval cat and a jackal all at the same time. These three animals used to go out together and the leopard would catch food for the jackal. When they're young they accept each other but as soon as they get older hormones start kicking in and instinct comes out and the animal that was his friend might well become his dinner.

"Cats, like lions, are predictable to a certain degree. The higher the intelligence of an animal the lower the instinctive value," says Ian. "For example, with the lion having a lower intelligence he has greater instinct and a lot of times in play that instinct will kick in."

We have faced a lot of jealousy and criticism about our projects. But if one thinks that we started from nothing and have really worked hard to get where we are and have saved so many animals it surely should stand for something. Some wildlife authorities feel that an animal not with its mother doesn't have a chance of survival. We have had tremendous success with raising orphans. The only animal that does not successfully return to the wild is the lion. Once they have been hand raised they will always want to associate with humans so they are a potential danger to humans. It has happened that hand-raised lions have killed people. If a person runs away from a lion it becomes prey and the lion will give chase so the lions that we raise go into the breeding programme but their offspring will be wild and will be released.

There will always be people who object to any form of intervention. What they need to understand is that throughout the world man has destroyed the habitat of the wild animals. Man is the biggest reason for everything that has happened in the world – pollution, ozone depletion and so many other things. What are we actually doing to rectify things? There are many armchair conservationists who sit and point fingers but have they done anything for conservation? People who have actually seen our work have praised us for it and we have a deep seated belief in our efforts. The knowledge and experience that we have gained has made us so much more aware of animals, their needs and their social behaviour. It has enlightened us. The knowledge and understanding of animals that we've gained over the years must be passed on from generation to generation for the benefit of humankind and animals alike. We put tremendous pressure on wildlife as a direct result of humanity's population explosion throughout the world – wildlife will be the biggest losers unless we, as humans, become more proactive.

Some of our orphans

Ala's Story

Elephants

Elephants are very intelligent. They can think and override a lot of their instincts. Actually, its instincts are fairly low. You can tame an elephant and it will remain gentle towards you for life.

Becky and Tembo were about two years old when we got them from the Kruger National Park – they were orphaned from an elephant cull. In the beginning they were extremely aggressive. They just wanted to kill everyone. They had been through a traumatic experience. They witnessed their family being shot in a cull. It was something they would probably never forget. They charged with such unbelievable aggression. Once they charged Chris and threw him about a half a metre into the air. We won over their trust by continually being with them and they became the most tame animals. They used to follow us around.

Because they are herd animals they thought of us as part of their herd. We spent a lot of time with them and they tamed down fantastically. It's just that the bigger they get the heavier they get and they can be a little clumsy at times. If they run towards you it is wise to get out of their way because they are unable to stop in time. These particular elephants were so tame that one could lie on the ground and they would walk over you and not hurt a hair of your head. They are called the gentle giants.

We had a stray elephant break in from the Kruger Park. Becky had reached the age when she was ready to have young. Elephants have a fantastic way of communicating (called infrasound). They can communicate over quite a distance with sounds that we can't hear. This stray elephant came along with two other bulls. But he alone stayed and joined Becky. We called him John Slade, after Janusz's friend who stole his wife. Tembo was put out (unlike Janusz). He was used to being the boss and now Becky had turned her attentions to another elephant. His nose was really out of joint and he became a bit of a delinquent. He used to take his frustrations out on the lodge. He would come into the lodge grounds at night, rearrange the gardens, break water pipes and push the odd car over. He knew he was doing wrong because the minute he saw us he'd take off and just disappear. He was so clever he would anticipate his pursuers movements or the direction they would take and he knew that when he was discovered breaking in all he had to do was run to the first thick bush and stand completely still and the rangers would walk right past him because you cannot see elephants at night. We used to run ourselves sick and all the time he would be hiding and waiting for us to go somewhere else. He ended up breaking into the lion camps. He would knock down the gates and just walk out again. He was doing this night after night. As soon as we found a way of preventing his breakouts he would find a new way in. He was the best electrician and mechanic when it came to breaking electrified fences. It shows the intelligence of the elephant. Tembo was crying out for attention.

Tembo broke out of Tshukudu when Ian was monitoring him and decided to visit a store some distance away. According to the irate report received, the unruly elephant had actually broken into the shop. Unfortunately the tracking apparatus had stopped functioning. Ian finally reached the store to find that Tembo had caused pandemonium further up the road – a construction camp had been raided and its workers had taken refuge in the bush. Tembo knew he wasn't supposed to do this. He went into the neighbouring area, Balule, where Ian found him. Ian then read him the riot act and told him that he had been a very bad elephant. Ian was convinced that Tembo listened to what he said. Ian and Ross spent about three weeks constantly monitoring the recalcitrant animal. He would go in to camps when no one was there, trash the camp and steal anything he wanted. It turned out to be quite expensive as we had to pay for the damage of a bird book as well as many other things. We had to have a guard with him at all times because they threatened to shoot him and that's when we gave him to the Elephant Back Safaris. Now he's doing a fantastic job. He works near Tzaneen and helps to raise

Tembo and Becky with Ian, Chris, Lolly and Ala

Ala's Story

funds so that more elephants can be trained. They use hormones on the males to prevent them from coming into a state of musth. When a male elephant comes into a state of musth he gets extremely aggressive. They need to suppress the high testosterone level to make him really safe. He's having a good life. Elephant Back Safaris is another way of educating people who may otherwise never experience elephants at close range. In the case of Tembo the only other option was to destroy him. It was a compromise but has proved such a success.

Becky lost her first baby which was killed by a rhino during a drought. After her baby's death Becky went through a traumatic time. I was really touched, as I could see an almost-human behaviour. She went back to the where her baby died and was mourning her loss. She first tried to raise her dead baby by picking it up with her tusks. When she finally realised it was dead, she proceeded to cover its body with grass and branches.

Becky used to hang around near the lodge, crying to herself. The rangers used to go out and talk to her, keeping her company so she wouldn't be all alone and trying to reassure her, which she seemed to appreciate. We felt we had to get another elephant to keep her company. After negotiating a donation, we organised to get two from Karongwe Game Reserve. We captured them and brought them back. When Slade first came here he was an aggressive creature. Becky always used to come between us and Slade. If he threatened to charge she would lead him away. She did the same with the new elephants – always intervened. When the males were docile she would allow them to get close to us but otherwise she would run off and get them to follow her. Now the new bulls are getting really tame and we can even touch the younger one. We still need to be very careful because if they come into musth they could be dangerous and would need to be avoided. Becky now has a baby, Malutka. She's rather naughty and likes to chase and terrorise buffalo and other animals that tend to get too close.

Walking with animals

Walking with animals is unique to Tshukudu. It makes us very special. People are able to go out on game drives and be with animals in their natural environment and experience interaction by being able to touch a lion or other wild creatures. A lot of people come just for this. We have encountered a lot of disapproval about it but we put that down to jealousy because we have made such a success of what we've started. Very recently a lady came to me and said, "I cannot tell you what a wonderful experience it is to be here. Have you ever got things right!" This is only one example of the glowing reports we get and the complimentary things people write in our visitors' book.

The walks also serve the purpose of being an educational tool as well as allowing guests to interact with our orphans. Once Ian took a group of thirteen children from a high school in one of our rural areas. They were initially terrified of the animals. Many of them came from disadvantaged homes where they do not even keep pets at home. Some were more terrified of Ian's dog than of the lions! They walked down to the dam where Becky and her young elephant were with the other male elephant, rhinos and some buffalo. All these animals are in the 'Big Five' group. Savannah and one of the young lions had accompanied them on the

The lion cub with its friend in Sylvia's nursery

hike. The group began to walk home but Becky decided to join them. There they were thirteen children, Ian, Becky, her baby, the dog, the cheetah and the lion all walking in convoy through the bush. Maybe at the time the experience did not make a tremendous impact but in retrospect I'm sure they said, "Wow! We actually touched a cheetah and a serval cat and we interacted with Becky."

We try to eradicate the fear these children have of animals and replace it with respect. We keep in mind that these are still wild animals and capable of biting and scratching just like any wild animals so they must learn to treat them with understanding and respect. Before each walk the rangers give visitors instructions on how to behave when they encounter wild animals. It is only when people do stupid things like pulling ears or tails that one has accidents. We try to let them, to enjoy the 'awe' experience. We want them to have memories of how thick the skin of the elephant is and that the soft looking hair of the lion is really coarse to the touch. We feel that going on a walk with animals is a privilege and a time when one can share their space and environment, be accepted by them and form bonds.

Dealing with people

Our staff is very important to us. Ross has been here for over ten years. He was a ranger from KwaZulu-Natal. He's a really enthusiastic person. His wife, Sandy, came to us as a hotel student. She was a very quiet person and I didn't realise that there was something serious between them. They married in White River.

They both contribute more than I ask them to – that's devotion. Ross feels that the wonderful thing about working at Tshukudu is that it's not like a job but a way of life. He feels privileged to be there. It may not be his farm but he is passionate about the place. It is where we have tried to make him feel like one of the family and where he met his wife.

Like us, Ross believes that if there is a possibility of rehabilitating and saving an animal we need to try. He also values the incredible relationships that they

Ross and Sandy's wedding, with family including Lolly, David, Patrick, Sylvia, Ian, Chris, Steven, Richard, Sonja, Matthew, Jessica and Ala Sussens; plus Sandy's mom, Heidi Hutter, Wendel and Patsy (centre back), Chris Vink (behind Ross), Pat Tweedie (centre front) and Des Soule peeping out from behind Sandy with Mike Donnison and Marianne Wilding behind her

Ala's Story

build up with the animals. He always warns, however, the great need for respect for the wildness of the animals we deal with. Ross's favourite animal is the White Rhino. He describes it as: "A gentle, beautiful, agile creature who doesn't want to harm anyone." We may not all agree with his description, but we value his sincerity and passion.

A person whom Ross always loved and admired was Pat Tweedie. She visited Tshukudu so many times, six weeks in February and six weeks in October. She starts to plan her next trip as soon as she returns to England. She epitomises the kind of person who keeps returning to us.

Wendel is our 'professor'. He has a degree in teaching which stands him in good stead when with a group of guests. He is our head ranger. He loves the animals and is dedicated to his work. We are so lucky to have him and his wife, Patsy, here.

Wendel feels that Tshukudu has successfully recognised the need to change the role of the game ranger from the original fellow on horseback making sure the animals are all safe to the person who enables an enjoyable, directed experience being with animals. He says, "When people join the staff Ala always says: 'You either become one of the family or you won't last long.' " This is true. They do become part of our extended family.

He and his wife have worked here for many years and presented us with two "Tshukudu" babies. We have had many other devoted rangers throughout the years.

Des Soule was also another special person at Tshukudu. She was more than an employee. She was my right hand and my soulmate.

Most people who visit Tshukudu are wonderful. They arrive as our guests and leave as our friends. We have, however, had our share of surprising visitors. Chris once had a group of people staying in his tent camp. One lady decided not to go on a game drive with her husband and spent the afternoon in their tent. On his return the lady picked a fight with her husband and they seemed to be trying to kill each other. They did considerable damage to the tent. Chris asked Ross to come to his assistance and he was forced to handcuff the lady in order to restrain her. We took her to the lodge and put her into one of the cottages and kept a night watchman nearby in case she broke out. The next day her husband had to hire a taxi to take her back to Johannesburg because she couldn't travel with him. It was sad really because there was also a little boy of about nine who kept saying that his mother was possessed and asking his father to leave her, to divorce her.

Another 'people' experience cannot be written off as just an unpleasant incident, but has made a much deeper impression. Two people arrived from Spain and interviewed Chris. They claimed to be agents, but had hidden cameras. They told a story about a man who was crippled and dying of cancer and had a wish to shoot a lion. They thought that Chris might be able to tranquilise one of the lions in the breeding camps and the man could shoot it from a vehicle. Of course it was a trick but Chris replied, "I can't help you, but if you want something like that you should go to the Free State. I do not do that kind of hunting."

They returned to Spain and fiddled with the tape so that it sounded as if Chris was willing to do what they had asked for at a price. They had planned it really well. The scheme had been initiated by an international fund for animal welfare. These are guys that go around all over the world supposedly to highlight the plight of the animals. They claim that all the money that they raise goes towards assisting animals but it's a bit like people who make money out of religion. It appears to be a front for something a little more sinister. This same group was also involved in the Cites issue where they wanted to ban the sale of elephant products. What happens if you do this is that you create a huge market for banned goods. The price becomes inflated and provides an incentive for people who are living below the breadline to break the law.

The international organisation had instigated a campaign of discrediting lion breeders and, to give them their due, there are lion breeders who are involved in

Janusz and I on holiday in Australia

Ala's Story

unhealthy practices. But all they did was to discredit breeders who are legitimate. We never allow hunting in our camps, but what they did hurt all of us. They actually took a photo of our gate with our name and broadcasted it on television. The implication was that our practices were bad. The way in which it was presented implied that we were the only people who did these awful things. When we appealed against it they blocked out the name 'Tshukudu' in their second screening but the damage was done. We had no recourse to sue for libel or loss of patronage. It would have cost a fortune which we did not have. We appealed to the Independent Broadcasting Commission but we were up against a powerful organisation. Ian went on a radio talk. I suggested that the interviewer ask them what this organisation did with their money. He replied that if he did that he would be out of a job the next day.

Unlike the other international organisation, WWF do wonderful work with the money they raise and we continue to support them. Every cent they get goes into wildlife conservation.

I suffered emotionally after the lion controversy. We have been in conservation since the Livingstone days – and were privileged to travel throughout Europe, Australia, the Far East, Alaska and Canada, experiencing first hand the 'best practice' conservation methods around the world. We plowed every available cent we had into Tshukudu – and now this! My friends were very supportive at the time but I needed to get away, to restore my soul. With the help of friends and family and my faith in God I was able to pull through.

Part 5

Back to the beginning

September – October 2004

Ala's Story

The return

In October 2004 we were invited to visit Poland as part of a group of people who had all been deported to Siberia as children. Initially I did not want to return to the place of my birth because of my deep-seated fear and hatred of communism which I believed had over-run the country. In 1989 I had returned to find devastation. It broke my heart to see Poland in shreds and its people without spirit. The destruction wrought by communism was awful to see. It seemed as if the energy of the people had been sapped and the physical destruction was evident in the derelict buildings. I found it incredibly sad. At the time I had wanted Lolly to see my homeland but it was a mistake. I returned to South Africa disillusioned and vowing never to return. As time passed people came back from Poland with stories of how things were changing and that I should revisit the country to see it for myself.

The invitation came from Stefan Adamski, one of the 'orphans' from Oudtshoorn. He asked if I wanted to join the group but because of my reservations I made excuses, one of which was that Janusz would be visiting from Australia at that time. My pretexts were not to be accepted. Basia, the organiser, phoned and said that she had cancellations so why didn't I bring Janusz along? My brother and I had spoken about returning to Poland. We were both getting older, so our time for travelling might soon be over and we felt that we would love to see it just once more. I contacted Janusz and he said that he would like to go and then Lolly decided that he too would enjoy the trip. We would be celebrating our 50th wedding anniversary while in Poland so I was really happy that Lolly would be there. This turned out to be a different kind of experience to the one I'd had on my previous visit under a communist government .

The tour group consisted of 34 people most of whom had experienced Siberia. Many of them were orphans who had ended up in Oudtshoorn. We met in Warsaw on a Monday morning. It was just wonderful. The streets had been rebuilt, people looked smart and weren't dressed in black as they had been on my previous visit. Most of the buildings had been restored and the palaces were there to be seen in all their splendour.

We were taken to Pryszkow where the whole group was staying – about 60 kilometres from Warsaw. The following day we visited the capital as a group. At dinner I was delighted to realise that the lady who had been my bridesmaid was sitting opposite me. I didn't know any of the others; we were from so many different walks of life. However, I made some good friends in the group during the tour.

While in Warsaw, Andrzej, a friend of ours, met us to assist in getting visas to go to Lithuania. The region of Poland in which I had been born had been ceded to Lithuania after the war. Andrzej took us to the embassy after which we rejoined the group at midday. This was to be a very special moment. We met at the palace in a ballroom which had been beautifully restored and redecorated. It was the launch of a book called 'Children From Siberia'. Of course I bought one and it is a very thick book which I carried everywhere I went. I discovered a picture of myself in the book which I found really emotional. At the launch there were people from all over the world, even consuls representing different nations and there were many speeches. The Polish army band played songs and mine were not the only tears flowing. It was a lovely occasion. The lunch only started at 5pm. In Warsaw there is also a Polish Polonia house (a Polish club). Here they welcomed us with CDs of Polish songs, books on Poland and speeches by those in charge. We felt that we were being treated like royalty.

The following day we visited Warsaw again and were invited to the Senate where we met the vice marshal of senate, a very charming lady who had visited South Africa. Needless to say Janusz had his photograph taken with her and afterwards told everyone he had been holding her behind while the photo was being taken. "I was too!" quips Janusz, "And what's more she didn't seem to mind it at all."

The minister talked about what we meant to the Polish people and congratulated us for what we had done with our lives. After that we went to parliament. We sat at the back and listened to a bit of discussion and then we were taken to a restaurant near parliament. We were joined for lunch by various important officials. I showed them our brochure on Tshukudu. They seemed delighted by it and asked many questions. After lunch we were given gifts of crystal ornaments and returned to our hotel loaded with presents.

The next day we visited a place called Chestochowa. This was absolutely stunning. We had a charming guide named Bella. Again we were so well cared for. We were reminded of the words of Polish songs, lots of them very sad about soldiers going to war and the life and history of Poland.

We also visited many churches in fact Stefen was concerned that Basia, our guide for the churches, was trying to turn us into saints. There was one very memorable church in Chestochowa, a really beautiful one on the way to Krakow where there is an altar of the Black Madonna protected behind steel railings. The church is filled with crutches and wheelchairs left behind by people who have been miraculously healed. There are also tokens of their gratitude in the form of jewelry and other gifts. People walk around the altar on their knees. Once inside the church a mass was said for us. Janusz was overcome with emotion.

"I've only cried twice in my life and one time was in this church in Poland."

Everywhere we ate we were served Polish food – food I remembered from my childhood including *pierogi*, a dough with a filling of mince, plums, cabbage or strawberries, either sweet or savoury. When walking in the streets we came across vendors selling pierogi which we bought and couldn't get enough of.

From Chestochowa we travelled down towards Krakow. On route we stayed at the Chopin hotel which is in Krakow and is very beautiful with so much character. In the streets there were buskers playing violins and singing. There were also many stalls selling a great variety of things. It is such a colourful place. One could spend hours wandering around looking at the restaurants, hotels, and shops. The cobbled streets made me realise just what an old and beautiful city this is. We spent two days there.

In all the time we were there I only came across one woman who was rude. Apart from her the people in Poland were friendly and kind.

From Krakow we went to Zakopane which is in the mountains. This was the first time we could enjoy a rest. Up to this point we had really been on the go. We had visited churches and palaces and climbed on and off busses at least fifty times. In this mountain paradise we stayed in a comfortable little guest house. The owner had saved money mostly by trading back and forth in Germany until she had accumulated sufficient funds to buy this beautiful place.

From the guest house one could take a raft down some rapids. It was a journey of about two and a half hours. I didn't go because it was too cold. The town itself was lovely. I said to Janusz that if I had to go to live somewhere other than Tshukudu I would choose this charming village. The people were very friendly and wanted to know all about South Africa. They were also extremely industrious. One gentleman I met ran a confectionary shop. He supplies one hundred and forty restaurants in Poland. He employs a hundred people. Previously there were no business enterprises as everyone worked for the state. What progress!

We also saw people who are still struggling. Farmers have to do all their own work. The elderly farmer's wives had to cut the grass so that their cows have food for the winter. When we visited a farm we took food for the farmer's dogs. The couple chatted with us and did not want to let us go. We also went for walks in the beautiful countryside.

We returned to Pruszkow and stayed in a castle on a hill that has been turned into an hotel – what luxury. We were treated wonderfully.

Everywhere we went we were given presents. Once we were all given loaves of bread which is considered to be a welcoming gift and a popular custom in Poland. We unfortunately had to give away our bread but the people were amazing. There was so much love everywhere we went.

The tour came to an end. It was sad to say goodbye. We'd had lots of fun and lots of vodka. Even I had a little tot. Lolly and Janusz had their sessions every night in the room which put them in a great mood for the evening but left them feeling not too good the next morning. Everyday in the bus we were offered something different – Polish vodka, Polish fruit, bread or chocolates. Wherever we went we were fed by one of our group, a chap from Richards Bay, South Africa, who spends six months of each year in Poland helping the farmers. He bought the stuff and we all shared it.

We spent one night in Warsaw where we hired a car so that we could visit cousins. Driving in Poland is so different to travelling in South Africa. We had estimated our travelling time but it took us twice as long so were forced to spend an extra night on the road. Because of my miscalculation as to the time it would take for us to reach her, my cousin became worried when we did not arrive. She thought we could have had an accident and she phoned every police station in the area to find out if something bad had happened.

It had been 14 years since I had seen my cousin Lila. She looked well. Her husband had bought her a little flat in an old building. She lives a simple life. I asked her how things were. She said, "You cannot believe how wonderful things are. You can't compare it to what it was like 14 years ago."

I was struck by the fact that our family had been forced apart. When I saw my cousin all my memories came flooding back. Lila used to stay with us. We had so much to talk about but there was also so much sadness. She wanted to hear everything about my mother and what had happened to us since leaving Poland. Our time was short but also very special. She has so little but she made such a huge effort for us.

We then moved on to Turek to visit another cousin, this time a relative of my father's. Once again we were astounded by the hospitality. The cousin, Grazyna, is 92 and her daughter, Wanda, did all the work. Both were so excited about the

Janusz, Father and I as children in front of our house

visit that they had hardly slept for a week. The whole town knew that we were coming. One man donated three kilograms of chocolate and refused to let them pay anything towards it. The dining table was laden. Grazyna's two granddaughters were also there. One lives quite near by but the other had to drive four hours to be with us. One is a judge and the other a lawyer. Love and joy! They would not let us go and we talked until about three in the morning. When I later phoned the cousin to thank them Wanda said, "Two months ago we celebrated the marriage of one of my daughters and it was a memorable experience, but last night, talking to you was something that I will never forget." Wanda wanted to drive to Warsaw but I persuaded her not to. She did, however, pack food for our journey. There was so much that in the end we had to give it to the maid who cleaned our room.

From Turek we flew to Wilno. Apparently flying was better because there were so many delays on the roads especially when going through customs.

When we had booked our flight the lady in the ticket office asked why we were going to Wilno. We told her we wanted to find the house where we were born. She asked if we had made any arrangements for accommodation there. She said that she had a good friend in the Polish airlines who would be able to help us. At the office we met this lady who organised a chauffeur-driven car and agreed to book us into our accommodation. She found us a guest house. She spent two hours arranging the trip while Lolly patiently sat outside with the suitcases. We drove fifty kilometres to Swieciany. As we were driving we passed beautiful scenery, forests and lakes. Poland's forests have been preserved even in the middle of Warsaw. We also saw lots of prostitutes in the forest so we asked Janusz if we should drop him off in the forests. Most of the ladies came from Rumania and Bellarus. They are not allowed to ply their trade in the cities which is why they are seen there. The hundreds of truck drivers in Poland give them lots of business. They were all very smartly dressed.

As we drove through Swieciany I suddenly said, "Janusz, I'm not sure, but I think that's our house." I saw it from the road. I remembered a long alley from the main road. When we got closer we saw it was really our house. Needless to say it is in a sad state of repair. No one lives in it. The beautiful gardens are a thing of the past and there are many new buildings around it. Fortunately Janusz had brought a photo of us as children on the steps of the house in father's motor bike so we were able to make a positive identification.

We walked around the house and looked through the windows and I was extremely moved. I thought of our happy days and the wonderful memories I have of my parents and a special childhood but I had to shake myself and say, 'This is now'. After the war our house was turned into a police station, but now it just stands empty and forlorn, falling into a state of ruin. Of the experience Janusz says, "Watching Ala and feeling her emotions rubbing off on me was unbelievable."

Our old house as we found it on our visit

I phoned Renia to tell her that we had found the house and she immediately asked, "Have you seen the hills?"

The town was more built up than I remembered it and I wasn't too sure that the hills we saw in the distance were the same ones that we had sped down in the snow on our way to school. I wanted to see the railway station but a man told us that there was no railway station there only in the next town. This could have been the one we were taken to on the start of our journey to Siberia. In the morning we went to the church and we stood on the steps where Renia and I had posed for out photographs after our first communion.

We were very happy that we had been able to see the place of our birth although it had been emotional. I would never have planned that trip. It's strange how things worked out. I am an African now, but would be very happy to return to Poland for a visit.

So we end up where we began – with Janusz's obsession with sex, my concern and love for my brother, and my love for husband, sons and grandchildren who have always been there for me, to drive me if I need them and who demonstrate the value of family. Finally, we have come full circle – back to the place where I had been born.

I've had a super, fantastic life in Europe, the Middle East and in Africa, one that's been full of adventure, hard work, sadness, happiness, the joy and heartbreak of animals, love and friendships – but a life always guided by the Grace of God.

Postscript by author

This is a story about Ala's life experiences. It is a tale of the events that shaped her and made her the person she has become. Exiled as a child from her motherland she had to become a self-reliant adult at an early age. She opted to remain in a foreign country and overcame many obstacles with courage and fortitude.

In the book she has not dwelt much on her sons and her grandchildren although her love for them is always evident. The building up of Tshukudu had the interests of future grandchildren in mind – that they might have a place to grow up in, to flourish, learn about conservation and appreciate the privilege of a life close to nature. Since writing this book, Chris has married Vicky – and Ala welcomes Vicky to the family and wishes them a great and happy future together.

The birth of Ala's six grandchildren brought joy and a new sense of love and fulfillment to her life. They are the reason for putting her story into a book. She wanted to give them a history, a background as to who they are and what they should strive for.

Ala has started a tradition which she hopes will continue through her children and grandchildren. Maybe one day they, too, will have a story to tell.

– Dr Joan Duff, July 2007

Ala's Story

Words Ala Kuchcinska Sussens with Dr Joan Duff
Sub-editing Josef Talotta
Design BrandDrive
Maps (pages 90 and 126) used with kind permission of
Map Studio, Cape Town – www.mapstudio.co.za
Printing Colors, Johannesburg

Tshukudu Game Lodge
PO Box 289, Hoedspruit 1380
Limpopo, Republic of South Africa
Tel +27 (15) 793-2476 or (15) 793-1886
Fax +27 (15) 793-2078
E-mail tshukudugamelodge@radioactivewifi.co.za

www.tshukudulodge.co.za

ISBN 978-0-620-39915-9